RED DIRT COUNTRY

RED DIRT COUNTRY
FIELD NOTES AND ESSAYS ON NATURE

JOHN GIFFORD

UNIVERSITY OF OKLAHOMA PRESS : NORMAN

This book is published with the generous assistance of the Wallace C. Thompson Endowment Fund, University of Oklahoma Foundation

"Fires" was previously published in *Southwest Review* 100, no. 2 (2015).

"Oh, Give Me a Home . . ." first appeared in *The Smart Set*, January 11, 2017.

"It Nourishes You" was first printed in *Kestrel: A Journal of Literature and Art*, Fall 2017, and was a "Notable" selection in *The Best American Essays 2018*.

Library of Congress Cataloging-in-Publication Data
Names: Gifford, John Allen, author.
Title: Red dirt country : field notes and essays on nature / John Gifford.
Description: Norman : University of Oklahoma Press, [2019]
Identifiers: LCCN 2018051859 | ISBN 978-0-8061-6330-7 (pbk. : alk. paper)
Subjects: LCSH: Oklahoma—Description and travel. | Human ecology—Oklahoma. | Nature—Effect of human beings on—Oklahoma.
Classification: LCC F701 .G54 2019 | DDC 304.209776—dc23
LC record available at https://lccn.loc.gov/2018051859

The paper in this book meets the guidelines for permanence and durability of the Committee on Production Guidelines for Book Longevity of the Council on Library Resources, Inc. ∞

For Mom and Dad,
and Paul, Matt, and Jenny

CONTENTS

ACKNOWLEDGMENTS

Grateful acknowledgment is due the editors of the journals and magazines in which essays from this volume originally appeared: Willard Spiegelman and Jennifer Cranfill, *Southwest Review*; Byshera Williams and Melinda Lewis, *The Smart Set*; and Donna J. Long, *Kestrel: A Journal of Literature and Art*. I thank these editors for supporting my work. Also, I offer my gratitude to those who were kind enough to share with me the results of their research and scientific study, which enhanced my understanding of some of the subjects addressed in *Red Dirt Country*. This includes Richard Minnich at the University of California, Riverside; Josie Galbraith from the University of Auckland, New Zealand; and James Guldin of the U.S. Forest Service. Special thanks go to Justin Roach, Kyle Troxell, and Joanne Ryan of the U.S. Fish and Wildlife Service; to my friend and former teacher Susan Kates at the University of Oklahoma; and to Rondi Large of WildCare in Noble, Oklahoma, an organization doing wonderful work in rehabilitating injured and orphaned wildlife. My sincerest gratitude and appreciation go to Andrew Furman of Florida Atlantic University, and to Oklahoma's 2017–18 poet laureate, Jeanetta Calhoun Mish of Oklahoma City University, for reading an early version of *Red Dirt Country* and offering suggestions that helped improve this book. Additionally, I'd like to thank Louisa McCune, Gladys Lewis, Nels Rodefeld, Ed Godfrey, Bryan Hendricks, Jonathan Starke, Valarie Thorpe, Lee Gutkind, Lisa Springer, and the Reverend Al Poteat, all of whom have, in one way or another, encouraged my work as a writer over the past twenty-two years. I thank the University of Oklahoma Press, particularly editor Kathleen Kelly, for supporting this project. And, as always, I'm most grateful to my wife, Ellen, and son, Jackson, for their love and encouragement each and every day.

 RED DIRT COUNTRY

INTRODUCTION

On a recent warm summer evening, my wife and I enjoyed a walk in Heritage Hills, Oklahoma City's grand neighborhood of stately, century-old homes and its forest of mature trees, just north of the city's bustling Midtown district. At one point I noticed what appeared to be a pecan lying in the street, and I picked it up. It was still encased in its thick green hull. Nearby was another, much larger, pecan. It too was ensconced in a soft, leathery husk. I assumed some frolicking squirrels had knocked these nuts from their trees, whose sprawling branches arched over the surrounding lawn and adjoining sidewalk, reaching their terminus above the street. The nuts had some heft to them, especially the larger one. As a kid, I would have relished the opportunity to hurl them at something. All I wanted now, however, was to take them home and study them. We were still months away from the pecan harvest, when the brittle hulls would split open with the first few frosts, dropping the ripe nuts to the ground, and for this reason I wanted to know how far advanced the kernels of these pecans were. Judging from the size of the hulls, they appeared fully developed, or very near it. But what did the nuts themselves, their kernels and shells, look like at this point? I planned to slice them open and investigate. Then I decided it might be more interesting simply to watch them and note how they changed from day to day now that they were separated from the tree.

The hulls were soft, smooth, and solid green when I brought them home, but each day thereafter I noticed some subtle, and other not so subtle, changes. For one, they gradually darkened, developing irregular brown or black patches on their surface, very much like a banana. Also, dark lines formed along the seams where the hulls would have eventually opened to release their contents, while the hulls themselves gradually dried and became more withered each day.

After several days I realized something interesting: the hulls were beginning to resemble the pecans themselves. That is, they were developing these dark patches and lines, which seemed to replicate the shell, and thus the appearance, of a mature pecan. Yet, like a human too soon separated from his family, perhaps finding himself out on the streets with no love or support, these pecans were hardening, though undoubtedly hollow and undeveloped on the inside.

Although the U.S. Department of Agriculture, as well as most growers, shellers, processors, distributors, and consumers, considers pecans "nuts," they're actually something called a "drupe," a seed-containing "stone" or pit, covered by a fleshy substance. The difference is that with most drupes, such as apricots or mangoes or cherries, we eat the succulent flesh while discarding the pit and inner seed. With pecans, it's just the opposite. We eat the seed, the kernel, while discarding the shell and never noticing the protective hull except when the entire unit separates from the tree and falls to the ground, requiring us to crack it open in order to access the nut within.

Each day I've continued to notice gradual but distinct changes in my two pecans. The hulls have even developed fine points on either end, just like the pecan shells themselves, although by now they're past the point of looking like nuts. They've continued to darken as the hulls have dried and withered. I'm very interested to know what they'll look like a month from now. Will the hulls become so dry that they'll open up on their own, as in the wild?

Or will I have to crack them to access the pecans? And what of the pecans? How developed, or stunted, are the kernels? The shells? Time will tell. Time, and careful observation.

Over the years I suppose I've conditioned myself to look not only at the proverbial forest, but also, and perhaps more importantly, at the individual trees, and their leaves, and the shape and pattern of a single leaf, how it's attached to its stem, to its branch, and how the trunk itself is rooted into the earth. Like animal tracks on a riverbank, each detail is a clue to something larger and more significant, and over time the slow accretion of these details tells a story, nature's story, which is playing out every day all around us.

"The question is not what you look at," wrote Henry David Thoreau in 1851, "but what you see."

In his *Journal*, Thoreau (1817–62) recorded the details of such phenomena as the symmetry of a snowflake, the architecture of a muskrat nest, the story told by a fox's tracks. In his entry for August 19, 1851, he writes of exchanging a macrocentric view for the micro: "I fear that the character of my knowledge is from year to year becoming more distinct & scientific—that in exchange for views as wide as heaven's cope I am being narrowed down to the field of the microscope—I see details not wholes nor the shadow of the whole."

But what details this intense focus revealed. Consider his observations of a chestnut, for example:

> What a perfect chest the chestnut is packed in! With such wonderful care Nature has secluded and defended these nuts, as if they were her most precious fruits, while diamonds are left to take care of themselves. First it bristles all over with sharp green prickles, some nearly half an inch long, like a hedgehog rolled into a ball; the rest on a thick, stiff, bark-like rind, one sixteenth to one eighth of an inch thick,

which, again, is most daintily lined with a kind of silvery fur
or velvet plush one sixteenth of an inch thick, even rising in
a ridge between the nuts, like the lining of a casket in which
the most precious commodities are kept. The chest is packed
quite full; half-developed nuts are the paper waste used in
the packaging, to fill the vacancies. At last Frost comes to
unlock this chest; it alone holds the true key.

For Thoreau, there was something sublime in these details, something elusive to science, something that transcended simple fact
and knowledge and, in doing so, rendered life more meaningful.

"If there is not something mystical in your explanation," he
writes in his journal entry for December 25, 1851, "something
unexplainable to the understanding, some elements of mystery, it
is quite insufficient." He then adds, "If we knew all things thus
mechanically merely, should we know anything really?"

Imagine the inspiration Thoreau might have found in the
pecan had he been from the south-central United States. They're
no less perfectly packaged than the chestnut and infinitely tastier
than the acorns he wrote of eating. They're also one of nature's
most nutritious foods, and the trees that produce them grow wild
here on the southern Great Plains as they have for millennia.

Decades before Henry David Thoreau documented his
myriad observations of the natural world around Concord, Massachusetts, the Reverend Gilbert White (1720–93) was recording
intricate details of his native Selborne in Hampshire, England,
and reporting on these shrewd and erudite observations in his
correspondence with naturalists Thomas Pennant and Daines Barrington. These letters would eventually form the basis for White's
celebrated book *The Natural History of Selborne*, a classic of nature
writing and a case study on the power of close and careful observation, in both subject and scope. White believed that by focusing his

environmental vision on his own community, he could more fully understand it. His wish in publishing his book was that it might serve to inspire others to more carefully examine nature in their own communities.

"Men that undertake only one district," White pointed out, "are much more likely to advance natural knowledge than those that grasp at more than they can possibly be acquainted with: every kingdom, every province, should have its own monographer."

The Natural History of Selborne is filled with keen observations of bird behavior, insects, and weather patterns, and their effects on wildlife, local gardens, and the people of his rural village. It's a reminder of what we can learn when we train our eyes and minds on something specific, even something minute and seemingly insignificant, and allow it to reveal itself.

White's book helped inspire me to look more closely at the natural world in my own small part of the planet, on the southern Great Plains, in Oklahoma. And in doing so, I found myself intrigued by plants and animals and natural phenomena I thought I knew, but which I now realize I'd always taken for granted and thus never really understood. It wasn't enough that I'd cast my eyes upon these things day after day, year after year. Rather, it was an understanding that I'd never really seen them at all until their details became so dear.

The field notes and essays contained in this volume are the results of such concentrated and often sustained observation, and for this reason I'm fairly certain that if my fifth-grade teacher were to read this it would come as some surprise. *Why couldn't you focus like that in my class?* he'd wonder. If only our classroom had been outdoors, perhaps beneath a wild pecan, or on the shores of a shady stream surrounded by native flora and fauna.

I should point out that the content herein is not scientific, nor is this book intended for a technical audience. Rather, this is creative nonfiction for general and literary readers, combining research with personal experience and observation as a way of better understanding the natural world around us—which we often forget we're a part of—and as a reminder that the everyday choices we make typically have far-reaching consequences, here at home and around the globe.

Part I, "A Riparian Journal," contains essays and sketches based on my observations of a central Oklahoma creek, month to month, day to day, and sometimes hour by hour, for more than twelve years. Of all the different ecosystems here on the southern plains, the riparian corridors, those wonderful natural buffers of trees and other vegetation skirting our rivers and creeks, are the most special and inspiring to me. For one thing, they insulate our native waterways in verdant plant life, and this provides shade and cover for fish and other species that swim, walk, and fly. Thanks to their expansive root systems, riparian buffers help eliminate erosion and thus improve water quality, and they play a major role in maintaining the integrity of the stream banks themselves. Also, they concentrate birds and other wildlife for the food and shelter they provide. Aldo Leopold spoke to this in his book *Game Management* (1933), in which he writes that "game is a phenomenon of edges. It occurs where the types of food and cover which it needs come together." As riparian corridors constitute veritable woodland-grassland interfaces, providing food, water, and cover, it's no surprise they also attract and concentrate wildlife. This is the type of "edge-effect" Leopold described, and though his focus was primarily game species such as quail and pheasant, the same principles apply to nongame varieties.

In a developed area such as a city or suburb, where natural habitat is often compromised, riparian spaces are even more important, for they become vital areas of microhabitat and legitimate urban forests, which benefit not only native fauna but also human lives. Studies have shown time and again that our own quality of life improves markedly when we live close to trees and other green spaces. And as we continue to develop our natural lands, as we pave more streets and parking lots and driveways and shopping centers, our increasingly fragmented green spaces assume a greater burden (and importance) in absorbing runoff after prolonged rainfall. This makes our riparian corridors vital for their ability to filter this excess, and often polluted, water, and to help maintain the structural integrity of the streams themselves, which serve to drain the larger watersheds and divert runoff that might otherwise prove detrimental to surrounding human communities.

While I've been fascinated by riparian areas all my life, it wasn't until my family came to live in a house whose backyard borders such a stream and urban forest that I was able to study and understand how vital these features are for both humans and wildlife. After a record-setting deluge some years ago, which Oklahoma's leading meteorologist called a "five-hundred-year flood," I realized it was the trees along my stream that had officiated the orderly evacuation of such a large volume of water and prevented most of my backyard from crumbling into the current and disappearing with it.

The essays in Part II, "Red Dirt Country," are meditations on various natural phenomena here in Oklahoma, many of which help elevate our own quality of life. These subjects include backyard wildlife, urban forests, and the annual summer migration of those elegant and graceful raptors, Mississippi kites. Also, this section explores our ongoing war with wildlife and the long-smoldering issue of wildfire suppression, which has plagued North American ecosystems for well over a century. And while fire suppression has, in the short term, helped protect our communities from flames, it has ultimately, and ironically, made us more vulnerable to them in the long run, a reality we see played out each year in the American West.

A May 5, 2015, article in *Wildfire Today* noted, for example, that in 1995 the United States averaged less than one "megafire" (a conflagration over one hundred thousand acres in size) each year. Between 2005 and 2014, however, this number increased to an average of nearly ten per year.

This surge in megafires is due in part to an unnatural accumulation of woody debris and other combustible materials in our forests. Some of these forests, despite being dependent on fire for their regeneration, haven't burned in over a century. Meanwhile, cities and suburbs continue to expand, swelling the human footprint on the earth and deepening our resolve to protect our communities from flames. But continued fire suppression is only exacerbating an already dangerous scenario. And the longer we deprive our forests and grasslands of periodic burning, the bigger and more destructive the fires will be when they do occur.

If this sounds like a recipe for disaster, it is. And it's already happening, not only here in Oklahoma but throughout the West.

In 2015, I interviewed Richard Minnich, PhD, a fire scientist at the University of California, Riverside, who told me that the buildup to today's larger, more destructive fires in his state began, not with recent droughts and the warming climate, but with fire suppression over a century ago. "The transition to fewer, but larger and more destructive California fires took place by 1920, after fire suppression began in 1905," he told me.

Here on the southern Great Plains, we can identify a similar correlation between large-scale European settlement in the late nineteenth and early twentieth centuries, and wildfire suppression. This in turn has led to the degradation of many of our natural landscapes, which imperils native wildlife communities. Consequently, it's no surprise that today, when conservation groups seek to revitalize places like the tallgrass prairie landscapes in northeastern Oklahoma, for example, they reintroduce not only bison to the land, but also periodic fire. Without it, the ecosystem is simply dysfunctional.

And yet despite overwhelming scientific evidence confirming the benefits of fire for our grasslands and forests, the subject remains politically combustible, fueled largely by misinformation. I could go on and on about it. But perhaps the reader has tired of all this hot talk. Grab your hat and let's go for a walk . . .

. . . and discuss urban wildlife and trees, and the special sustenance we humans derive from our natural surroundings. Part II contains several such essays. These pieces illustrate nature's uncanny ability to help us unplug from our increasingly hectic world and relax, recharge, and make sense of what's important. Collectively, these essays showcase the magic of close and careful observation while celebrating the energy, beauty, and vitality of the natural world that so improves our quality of life. They remind us that we're not mere spectators of nature, but rather part of the natural atmosphere that nourishes and sustains, and that our own lives improve in proportion to the health of our rivers and forests, mountains and plains.

I've had a lifelong fascination with the natural world and over the years have spent considerable time and effort studying, planning, and traveling to distant and sometimes remote land- and seascapes in which to immerse myself. And yet I've never learned more than when concentrating my focus on my home state, city, and even my own backyard, my private microcosm of the world at large. There is much to be gained from narrowing our field of view and looking more closely and carefully at the natural wonders all around us, not only because Gilbert White encouraged us to do exactly this, but also because the natural mysteries revealed to us in our home districts are as fascinating, and as worthy of our attention and scrutiny, as those exposed in faraway lands. What we discover might surprise us, revealing perhaps something at once universal and yet uniquely our own. For as Mary Austin writes in her inimitable classic, *The Land of Little Rain* (1903), "the earth is no wanton to give up all her best to every comer, but keeps a sweet, separate intimacy for each." To that end, shouldn't we all strive to better understand the landscapes in which we live, the plants and animals with which we share our planet, especially those in our immediate surroundings, which are most affected by our behaviors and actions, and whose vibrant lives are in many ways reflections of our own?

Studying the natural world around us is both enlightening and empowering. It's also a lot of fun.

PART I

A RIPARIAN JOURNAL

JANUARY

PRAIRIE SERENADE

I'm nearly asleep when the coyotes fire up across the creek, yipping and howling as they gather at forest's edge, rallying one another for the hunt to come, the pursuit of the food they seek. We might call this team building, establishing good working relationships with other members of our pack, building trust, building camaraderie, letting our peers know that come late or early light, we have their back. And so it is with the coyote, this remarkably intelligent canid that understands there is strength in numbers. The yipping begins as an erratic panoply of disordered notes before building into a concerted and spine-tingling crescendo of a family unit united in purpose and resolve, and fortified in camaraderie. My dogs look up, their ears erect, grateful their beds are indoors rather than in the backyard. My wife says the coyotes and their eerie howling give her the creeps. My father used to say these howling coyotes were his sentries. Whenever he heard them singing their prairie serenade, he said he was sure there was no one prowling about the fields and trees surrounding our home, or else the keen coyotes would have selected some other stage.

Unlike the wolf or the fox, the coyote is a product of America, having originated from a line of ancestral canids in the high deserts of the Southwest. All the while it has shadowed us, living on the outskirts of human society as it watched and learned and, in some cases, infiltrated our cities and towns and villages to reside among us. Although most would be quick to point out our differences, there is an unmistakable and remarkable symbiosis between humans and coyotes. Whether we realize it or not, we depend on them, not only to control populations of rats and mice and other pests, but also to remind us of our close connection to the land, and our own origins as hunters and gatherers, as bipedal omnivores. We see coyotes as symbols of the wild and particularly of the American West, and as icons of ourselves. Like humans, coyotes have proven their adaptability and resilience by extending their home range. From their native Southwest, they've moved south into Central and South America, north to the tundra, west to the Pacific, and they now roam our Atlantic shores. We've facilitated their expansion by eliminating their larger and more powerful rivals, wolves, from most of the North American continent. Coyotes have thrived in their absence.

These wild dogs have figured into American Indian culture for thousands of years. Our nation's earliest human residents viewed them as a deity figure, Coyote, yet shape-shifting and often beset with such human characteristics as greed and lust. In this, Coyote is reminiscent of the fox spirit in ancient Chinese folklore. A traditional Caddo folktale, for example, tells of women making corn mills from the trunks of old trees. While there were many such mills, there was one old and smooth tree trunk the women liked best. As women ground corn in the old mill, they began to see that the resulting cornmeal amounted to very little. After examining the mill, one of the women suggested they cut it down to see where the corn had gone. When they did, Coyote jumped up and ran away. He had transformed into a mill so that he could eat his fill of corn.

Despite decades of callous and relentless persecution from human society during the twentieth century, including federal poi-soning campaigns, helicopter-assisted shooting parties, trapping, and other tactics, coyotes continue to live among us today, stronger than ever, and indeed victorious in their ability to not only survive, but thrive. As such, they've again shown us something of ourselves, namely a tenacity and determination that are, ironically, the very ideals of the human spirit, reflected in our greatest achievements. We see this in our efforts to find a cure for polio, for example, and in our willingness and dedication to answering John F. Kennedy's challenge to send an American to the moon and return him safely to the earth. Coyotes might be earthbound, but they've colonized every corner of our country, including the densely populated Northeast and even our largest cities: Chicago, New York, and Los Angeles.

Growing up in central Oklahoma in the 1970s, I remember hearing coyotes on summer nights when my family would drive out of town, toward my grandparents' home in the country. Turning off the busy two-lane state highway, we would roll the windows down and let the warm air circulate through the car. As I recall, we never saw these elusive predators, but we could hear them singing from the fields and Cross Timbers forests skirting the country roads. Often, on winter nights when it was so cold and crisp outdoors, and perhaps wistful for the summer season that had passed, I would think back to our evening drives in the country and I could almost hear again the playful and energetic serenade of these wild canids. Hearing them today reminds me of those warm summer nights and the wildlife that prowled the shadows and moonlit fields just outside the city and beyond the edges of our car's headlights.

My family's home today isn't so far away from traffic lights, convivial restaurants, and busy four-way intersections. In fact, our subdivision, though once separated from downtown by several miles of fields and scattered forest, is still within the city limits. Given the ongoing development over the past twelve years, however, it has become a part of the city proper rather than merely an outlying housing community. Although the traffic and noise and human presence have increased exponentially during this period, the coyotes don't seem to mind. Even if they do, it hasn't impacted their ability to adapt and survive, to keep pace in their own way with human society and these rapidly changing times. We hear them often during winter, when their wild notes carry through the leafless trees and float across our creek late of an evening when all is cold and quiet and still. One chilly morning not long ago, I watched a couple of juvenile coyotes hunting along the edge of the creek that runs through my backyard. It was 8:00 A.M. and my neighbors were driving off to work and school, and in the distance I could hear the low garble of traffic out on the street. The coyotes had other things on their minds as they stalked along the bank, slipping through the trees and vines. Their movements were soft and slow, their ears erect as they trained their eyes and noses on the winding waterway below. Then my neighbor's dog began to bark and the coyotes melted into the creek and disappeared like snow on a warm, sun-exposed slope.

Lying here in bed, however, and listening to them yipping and howling less than a hundred yards from my window, I'm reminded that they're seldom far away. And for this, I'm grateful.

FEBRUARY

SPRING IN THE AIR

The daffodils in my backyard are beginning to bloom. The cardinals and mockingbirds are tuning out the chilly morning air and singing, celebrating, telling us spring will be here soon. Is winter over? I'm doubtful. In Oklahoma, often we see the harshest part of winter and the heaviest snows, if it snows at all, in March. This surprises many new residents to the state, but here on the southern Great Plains the weather is consistently fickle and predictably unpredictable. This year we've had hardly any winter at all, which is a blessing for those like me who thrive in warm weather. Yet a mild winter can also complicate things like bud break in our trees.

Many fruit and nut trees, such as the pecan, which is indigenous to our state, require a certain number of hours below forty-five degrees Fahrenheit in order to break down latent growth inhibitors in their buds. The number of these chilling hours varies considerably by species and location. Some trees may initiate bud break with only two hundred chilling hours over the winter season, while others may require six hundred hours or more. Most of Oklahoma's pecans are wild, or native, trees, each of which is genetically unique thanks to the pecan's cross-pollinating, or allogamous, nature. For an illustration of this, take a walk through a grove of native pecan trees in late autumn when the hulls are opening, releasing these precious nuts to fall to the ground. Though one tree may appear nearly identical to those surrounding it, it is genetically unique.

Take a look at its pecans. Each tree produces nuts of a different size and shape, and with different shell and kernel qualities. This is the pecan's natural survival mechanism, which ensures that a disease affecting one tree has little or no effect on the overall grove. It's an example of hybrid vigor, and it's the reason why wild pecan trees survived through millennia with no supplemental fertilizer or pesticides or other human input.

This genetic diversity can make for a rather uneven bud break schedule, and yet thousands of years of natural selection have leveled the playing field, so to speak, resulting in trees perfectly adapted to our specific climate. Trees exhibiting early bud break may be susceptible to late frosts, something that wouldn't affect a late-blooming tree. Conversely, a delayed bud break similarly delays pollination and limits the growing season, which over centuries, over millennia, could undermine the survival of the species. Mother Nature has it all sorted out, however, which is why wild pecan trees continue to thrive here in Oklahoma.

Pecan trees are one thing, but the birds flitting about and beneath the branches of the ash, walnuts, oaks, elms, locusts, and redbuds along my creek won't tolerate any delay in their spring. The cardinals are calling to one another. They seem on the verge of nest building. Ditto the mockingbirds, which are regaling us in their incessant medleys.

It used to be that the sight of robins on the lawn was a sure sign of spring. I recall, as a child, looking out my grandmother's kitchen windows on cool, sometimes cold, mornings in March and seeing robins foraging in her yard and knowing spring had arrived, regardless of winter's proclivity for lingering in some years. As our planet has warmed in recent decades, it's now common to see robins with us here in central Oklahoma throughout the dormant season. The robin in my backyard this morning must believe spring is here, for he's foraging in the way of all American robins: running across the lawn, pausing to look and listen, and then running a few more paces before stopping to peck at the moist soil and extract an earthworm from the ground. The robin repeats this maneuver another time or two before a red-bellied woodpecker, perched nearby, spies the robin's trick and flutters to the ground to have a go of its own. As it does so, the robin flies away to less contested territory and the woodpecker, suddenly alone and surrounded by the possibilities of satiation and contentment, begins pecking at the earth in imitation of its orange-bellied contemporary. The woodpecker, however, lacking the robin's precise touch, comes up short. Discouraged, and reminded perhaps that unlike the ground-probing robin, it is better suited for trees, the red-bellied woodpecker flies off toward the north.

The singing birds put me in mind of those I enjoyed listening to in Cuba a couple of weeks ago. I stayed in an old nunnery, which, while it had been updated and refreshed as a boardinghouse for travelers, continued to function as a working convent with a team of dedicated Catholic nuns. It was a beguiling and spacious structure in the heart of Old Havana, with a heavy wooden door separating its cool and calm interior from the busy pedestrians plodding over the ancient cobblestone street on its doorstep. Upon entering the convent, one comes upon an open-air courtyard, replete with tropical vegetation and surrounded by a narrow walkway and various rooms, and with arched doorways opening up onto quiet corridors leading off to intriguing spaces deeper within. Above this courtyard, on the second floor, is another walkway flanked by tall plastered walls, lavender in color, and doors opening into guest rooms, and, on the near side, by a wrought-iron fence reminiscent of those accenting the old Creole and Spanish architecture in three-hundred-year-old New Orleans, which was inspired of course by the breathtaking Spanish architecture here in five-hundred-year-old Havana and that of the ancient homeland across the Atlantic.

Sunlight warms the lavender walls of these upstairs rooms, and from the open air above one can hear voices from the street, the first of which, in the low light of early morning, are those of the mellifluous street vendors who come through, one by one, their warbling tenors and baritones offering fresh fruit, breads, and cheeses for but a few centavos. Later, midmorning perhaps, after the street vendors have retired to their quiet abodes and the echoes of their early-morning songs have long since evaporated into the warm air, when schoolchildren, businessmen, and pretty Cuban women appear on the street to begin their day, one hears, from this part of the convent, the nuns singing their hymns in worship while sharp-voiced background singers, the birds, feathered rainbows of every tropical shade imaginable, sing and whistle from cages hanging throughout the convent, offering praise for the brand-new day, and for the softening of the night sky as the sun slowly brings the old city to life.

MARCH

EVANESCENT IS THE SEASON

A writer from the East Coast remarked recently in an essay criticizing life in a certain southern Great Plains city that the redbud tree's only redeeming quality is its canopy of warm, pink flowers that appear for but a couple of weeks each year in early spring. He extended his reproach to include our area's long, hot summers, frequent droughts, and incessant wind, among other things. I can understand his frustration with the wind, but in his criticism of the eastern redbud—which is, incidentally, native to the East Coast—he neglected the context in which we experience the tree's profusion of color early each year, and that is through the thin and quickly dissipating cloud of dust kicked up by the retreating winter season as it moves off to terrorize the Southern Hemisphere. And this is invariably a source of joy and tremendous relief, for spring is here!

The mockingbirds who each year nest in one of my three redbud trees would challenge this essayist, for the tree has sheltered them through more than a few spring thunderstorms, which appear suddenly from the southwest and after a few intense moments, or perhaps several intense moments, rumble away toward Tulsa and eastern Oklahoma. When my family moved into our home some twelve years ago, there was a redbud seedling growing right outside my bedroom window. On windy nights it scratched against the glass, interrupting my sleep, so one day I removed the tree and replanted it at the edge of our woodlot in the far corner of the backyard, near the creek. Today it's taller than me. This redbud was highly appealing to the flock of cedar waxwings that migrated through our area last spring, those elegant eye-banded birds that combed the branches for bud and seed. I suspect they, too, would refute this writer's condemning screed.

The redbud's breathtaking pink canopy too soon loses its pizzazz, but this is part of its charm, for like blooming tulips and those few special weeks of idyllic weather prior to severe storm season, spring's most anticipated moments are ephemeral and too soon gone.

Here in Oklahoma, blooming redbud trees signify the spawning runs of white bass, which are leaving the reservoirs right about now and infiltrating rivers and streams. For anglers, this is one of the year's most highly anticipated events, and for good reason. White bass don't get very large, but they're tenacious feeders and spirited opponents on light spinning or fly tackle. Like the redbud's profusion of springtime color, these spawning runs don't last long, but they're full of life while they do. And like the redbud, which is our state tree, the white bass retains similar distinction here, for it's the Oklahoma state fish. Some believe this a curious choice. They wonder: Why not the ubiquitous largemouth bass? Or the genetically unique Ouachita-strain smallmouth bass of the Glover River? One can certainly make a case for these or others, but for better or worse, the white bass is our state fish, which isn't inappropriate. White bass—or "sand bass," as they're often called in Oklahoma—are open-water fish and during the warmer months they're nearly always on the move, chasing shad and other small baitfish all across our reservoirs. Their feeding frenzies are brief and intense, and memorable for those anglers fortunate enough to happen upon one. But it's their spawning runs that are truly special, and this is because they happen but once each year.

Some years ago, my friend Steve Boyd and I fished that

section of the Mountain Fork River above Oklahoma's most scenic lake, Broken Bow, with a local white bass fanatic named Main Hutcheson. Main was said to be a Lower Mountain Fork River Foundation board member who was also involved with the Trout Unlimited organization, but not long after meeting him Steve and I began to get the idea he would gladly give up trout fishing for the opportunity to catch white bass. And why not? As Main told us, "pound for pound, they have to be the best fighting fish in freshwater."

We boarded his flat-bottomed river boat and Main fired up the Go-Devil engine, guiding us upstream through a stretch of thin, boulder-strewn water. Thanks to the boat's shallow draft, we had no trouble negotiating this water, which would have posed a major challenge for a conventional bass boat or other deep-hulled vessel. Perhaps this explained why there were no other boats or anglers about, despite the white-bass run being in full swing.

As we made our way upstream, I spotted white bass chasing one another in the shallows. "What about here?" I said to Main, pointing to the fish we were passing.

"We're going after the big ones," he said. "Those are just little guys."

But they were fish. And they didn't look bad to me.

After a while we reached a deep pool well upstream of the lake. It was quiet and secluded. We had the river, at least this portion of it, to ourselves. In went the anchor. In went the flies—small minnow imitations. This time of year, in mid- to late March, the fish respond best to small flies and slow presentations, and this is what we offered. But even these flies were too large. After a few casts without a bite, Main suggested a smaller fly, of a chartreuse color. Steve wasted no time in tying one on. Using a six-weight rod and floating line, he began working the fly just beneath the surface while Main used a sinking-tip line to plumb the depths of the pool.

Soon, they were both into fish. I grabbed my camera and began snapping photos.

True to Main's word, these were large white bass, weighing between two and three pounds apiece. They took a minute or more to land. And interestingly, they were males.

Hutcheson told us that Broken Bow Lake and the upper Mountain Fork River are special white-bass fisheries because here the males of this species are as large as female white bass in other waters. At the time we were fishing, in mid-March, the big females had yet to move that far upstream. Main said this would occur when the spring rains raised the water level in the river. He said these females would run three pounds or more. That's impressive for white bass, a fish that even in small sizes puts up a respectable fight.

I've caught white bass on many Oklahoma lakes and in several streams across the eastern half of the state, usually not targeting them, but taking advantage of a sudden feeding frenzy on the surface while pursuing largemouth or smallmouth bass, or some other species. Even on those occasions when I did target them, such as during their spring spawning runs, for example, I couldn't recall catching white bass of such a uniformly large size. Clearly, the Mountain Fork had lived up to its billing as a choice destination for the white-bass run, but even here it lasts only a few weeks each year.

In this, it's not unlike our flowering redbud trees during spring, or our volatile and unpredictable weather in May, or the waves of birds that migrate through our state this time of year, regaling us in their color and life and purpose before vanishing overnight, heading off on their way, reminding us that we can't always count tomorrow that which is here today.

I remember Judy Farley, the forester I interviewed in 2004 for an article I wrote on forest-tower observers. At the time it seemed a dying profession, for whenever an Oklahoma Forestry Services tower observer retired or passed away, the position wasn't being refilled. Also, the observer's job, scouting for wildfires, was increasingly being performed by manned aircraft. Though Judy maintained that traditional tower observers were more cost-effective, and that southeastern Oklahoma was too vast an area to patrol with a single airplane, especially during fire season, which lasts from January through mid-April when conditions are typically dry, at the time I interviewed her, fifteen years ago—where has all the time gone?—Judy said the profession was dissipating like smoke in a breeze. "Our job is slowly being phased out," she told me. "Not long ago we had eight tower observers. Now we're down to four."

As of February 2018, the agency is down to one remaining tower observer who scans the surrounding forests for fire. And I'm told she's soon to retire.

EARLY BIRDS

It's 5:30 A.M. and a barred owl is hooting outside my bedroom window. *Who cooks for you? Who cooks for you?* This is answered immediately by another across the creek, and this exchange over who's cooking for whom, and perhaps who's eating, continues for fifteen minutes or more. I can't see the clock, but I know what time it is. The owls have been in this pattern of late. They begin hooting an hour, or sometimes a little more, before sunrise. It's time to start my day.

The barred owls are nesting now, and I suspect a quick walk through the woods would likely reveal a nest site in a tree hollow or snag. These raptors help keep our field mouse population in check, but the barred owl has also been known to take fish from a lake's surface, a behavior more closely associated with the kingfisher or bald eagle. The stomach contents of one specimen examined in the 1930s contained several crayfish, which underscores their adaptability.

Great horned owlets, on the other hand, have already hatched. Recently I visited the Tishomingo National Wildlife Refuge in Johnston County to see Oklahoma's champion pecan tree. The grand old tree is situated in a river bottom overlooking Cumberland Pool, a shallow freshwater estuary of sorts, fed by the Washita River. This area and its seasonal mudflats are a haven for snowy egrets, great blue and green herons, bald eagles, and a variety of shorebirds and other species. Not far from here, Justin Roach, the refuge's biologist who was kind enough to show me around the four-thousand-acre park, pointed to an owl's nest high in a pecan tree—not the champion pecan, but another large old tree, one of several in this river-bottom field, which collectively form something of a scattered grove of ancients. My unaided eyes couldn't see the nest, so Justin set up a tripod and spotting scope. Once he had it in focus, I peered into the viewfinder and found myself face to face with an adult great horned owl and a surprisingly hefty owlet. The mother's ear tufts looked to be three inches or more, and they fluttered in the warm March wind as she casually observed us through half-closed eyes. The youngster beside her seemed much more interested, however, as it peered down at us from the safety of its elevated nest, some sixty feet off the ground. Justin said the nest they were occupying had been constructed by a red-tailed hawk the previous year. I wondered whether this hawk had returned at some point to find its former nest occupied and, if so, what lessons it might have derived about the fleeting nature of things we often take for granted in our lives.

APRIL

THE NESTING INSTINCT

After my wife and I were married, we left apartment life behind and moved into our first house, a tiny 1940s-era bungalow with walls and windows so thin that all winter long we felt the chill of the cold north wind. Despite its energy inefficiency, however, we appreciated the house's midcentury design, its wooden floors, and spacious study. After two years here, we bought our first house, a small three-bedroom ranch that had been built during the Kennedy years and wired by the town's very best electrician, a man named Roy Valouch, whose name was stenciled on the stem wall inside the garage. I didn't care much for this house. It was old and badly outdated. But I took comfort in knowing that at least we wouldn't have to worry about electrical issues. In fact, I was so proud that Mr. Valouch had wired my house that when I painted the garage floor and stem wall, I left his neatly stenciled name and phone number just to remind myself of the home's provenance.

Before we moved in, my wife asked my father and brother if they'd open up the wall separating the living room and kitchen. They did, and afterward it was as if we'd jumped ahead to yet another house, so great was the difference this open floor plan made. With fresh paint in nearly every room, some new furniture, and a stainless-steel refrigerator, our home began to feel quite cozy. And not long after we moved in, our son Jackson was born.

This coziness was only temporary, however, and was soon

exchanged for convenience. After three years, it was off to another, larger home closer to our jobs. We lived here only three years before buying the home we've now owned for twelve. At the time, I had no idea we'd stay so long. A decade or more in the same house? Do people really do this? Until living here, I never knew what it felt like.

Our current home is convenient to the elementary school my son attended when we moved in. It's also much newer than any of our previous homes. It has sheltered us through floods, droughts, blizzards, extreme wind and hail events, and many ice storms. Though recently we've considered moving closer to my son's high school, we can't quite bring ourselves to let this place go. My wife loves our house, which we've improved considerably over the years with new floors and countertops and master bath. One of the reasons I'm reluctant to move is that I've come to appreciate the thin forest that skirts the creek running along one edge of our property. In over a decade here, I've seen dozens of animals in our backyard, ranging from rabbits and squirrels and raccoons to coyotes, foxes, and bobcats. But it's the birds I most enjoy, and twelve years in the same house have afforded me the opportunity to witness as many nesting seasons.

I remember as a boy being fascinated by the sparrows that would shoot like feathered rockets from the end of my grandmother's clothesline poles whenever I'd get too close. These poles were galvanized pipes, three or four inches in diameter, and every year the sparrows constructed their nests inside. It was a perfect location, or nearly so, for the pipes offered protection from everything except a curious kid with too much time on his hands.

The birds around my house today seem to prefer the fern basket my wife hangs on the back porch each April. She sets out two ferns, but only one gets attention from the birds—usually cardinals. This one is protected by the roof and suspended seven feet off the ground, well away from the nearest wall or brick column. It's a location that offers safety from predators and the weather, while the thick tangle of ferns conceals the nest itself. Our biggest challenge is the issue of watering. How do we keep the plant alive without disturbing the birds? We've found that they tolerate an occasional water hose slipped into the plant, though they object to any tampering with the basket itself and will streak away the moment we remove the plant from its hook. Some years, when the birds seem especially sensitive to our intrusion, we avoid watering the ferns for as long as possible. Without water, however, these plants don't last long in the Oklahoma heat, which undermines their suitability as nesting sites. Generally speaking, we've found it best to inconvenience the birds from time to time in order to maintain the viability of their nesting site.

Interestingly, the birds always gravitate to this particular fern, which, of the two hanging baskets we set out, offers the better protection. The other, which is more exposed to the sun and rain, is avoided each and every year.

As it is for our own homes, location is a vital point of consideration for nesting birds. Some species seek the most hidden and inaccessible sites. Others are more tolerant of traffic and noise and construct their nests surprisingly close to busy sidewalks, driveways, and doorways. In any case, only the birds themselves know exactly what they're looking for in a potential nesting site. And when they find a place to raise a family, I mentally mark that location and try to disturb it as little as possible.

Around the corner from my back porch, in the tall hedges on my home's sunny southern side, is a mockingbird's nest. Though I walk by it every week as I cut the grass, I never knew about it until the year I decided to trim the hedges away from the eaves. I saw the bird dart away as I cut into the first hedge, and it never returned that season. Fortunately, there were no eggs in the nest, though I still felt terribly for disturbing this cozy, hidden home. These days, I defer to the mockingbirds, whose eloquent singing and energetic antics I so enjoy. I simply accept the fact that my hedges are going to be overgrown and unkempt until late in the season, after the birds have left their nests.

Not long ago, a pair of wrens decided to make a home at the bottom of a large wreath my wife fitted to our front door. I watched the pair as they carried materials to the wreath and slowly created a small, bowl-shaped retreat. But invariably I would forget about it and open the door, scattering the birds. This happened three or four times before the wrens vacated the nest for good. I'm not sure where they're residing now, but I delight in seeing this pair on my back porch as they scour the bricks for tiny spiders and insects. There is something cheerful, if not comical, in these animated characters with their jutting tail feathers and bulbous physiques, their inquisitive and seemingly optimistic nature. Wrens are some of my favorite birds.

Living in the same house, in the same neighborhood, along the same creek, and among the same trees for twelve years has been so enjoyable. We've seen many different neighbors come and go, and a few of them stay. We've watched their children, and our own son, grow. We've watched the riparian forest behind our house gradually shade more and more of our backyard, the trees stretching higher and higher toward the sunlight they crave. And we've watched many different pairs of birds raise their young in nesting sites offering various levels of concealment, security, and convenience. In those years when we're slow to get the hanging baskets out on the porch, we've observed cardinals flying back and forth, fluttering around as if confused, obviously searching for that fern that worked so well the year before, much like our Mississippi kites, which often return to the same mature trees and use the same lofty nests each year. Our mourning doves, on the other hand, typically build flimsy nests fairly close to the ground and thus have to construct new homes, often in new locations, from season to season.

Of course, I may have failed to realize any of this had it not been for my family's ability to maintain the same address for so long. And for this I'm grateful, for our persistence has allowed me to witness nature's perfection.

Once, I watched from inside my house as a male cardinal attempted to demonstrate for its fledgling the fine art of foraging for insects and seeds. The youngster sat in the grass just beyond my window, seemingly unresponsive, uninterested, and unappreciative as his regal father pecked at the ground between them and, plucking up some morsel, showed the prize to the fledgling before spinning around and repeating the process. He did this again and again, as if to say, "See? This is how you look for food. This is how you survive out here when Mom and I aren't around to feed you."

Today I wonder whether it's this former fledgling or some other cardinal I'm watching flutter through the trees in my backyard. Perhaps it's this bird's offspring. And if we stay in our house another year rather than moving, perhaps we'll see this same parent preparing yet another new brood for the challenges of adulthood and sharing the rewards of choosing the right location in which to make a home.

MAY

A HARD RAIN

May 3: It's the sixteenth anniversary of one of Oklahoma's recent big tornadoes—locally known as the "May Third Tornado,"—which leveled part of the community of Moore, just south of Oklahoma City. No one who lived here at the time can forget it. I mention it because, here in Oklahoma, we have to pay attention to the weather. It's May, after all.

Today was sunny and a bit windy, but fortunately there was no severe weather. In fact, the last week has been beautiful—sunny and warm with temperatures in the high seventies and low eighties. My wife and I saw Bob Dylan in concert tonight, almost twenty years to the day I saw the Black Crowes perform in the city's Civic Center. The Black Crowes, which were then at the height of their popularity, were the first "big band" to stop in Oklahoma City after the 1995 bombing—another event that none of us who lived here at the time can forget. As I recall, the band donated all its earnings from that night to the city's recovery effort. Like the Black Crowes, Dylan was brilliant, his voice a gravelly growl at times and his band's steel guitar, with its Western sound, reminding me of the Oklahoma horizon, glowing orange and pink as the sun slowly sinks in the evening.

May 6: It's 1:00 p.m. and the sun has just come out from behind the clouds after a day—yesterday and last night—of heavy rainfall.

After seeing Bob Dylan in concert, and after listening to his second album, The Freewheelin' Bob Dylan, I keep singing his song "A Hard Rain's A-Gonna Fall." Maybe so.

Local meteorologists are saying all the ingredients are in place—upper-level wind shear, humidity, instability—for severe storms to form once the sun comes out to warm the atmosphere. Looks like this is already happening. Could be an active night. It is very windy today. Forecasters are cautioning viewers to remain "weather aware," which, while certainly not new in practice, seems to be the current catchword for keeping eyes to the sky.

At 2:30 P.M., western Oklahoma is under a tornado watch. I turn off the television and flip it on again an hour later. Now, at least two counties in southwestern Oklahoma are under a tornado warning, as radar and storm chasers have spotted "moderate rotation" in a storm near Chickasha. Later, a supercell thunderstorm forms in southwestern Oklahoma near the community of Apache and creeps northeast, roughly paralleling I-44, which it crosses twice before destroying much of the small community of Bridge Creek (which was also hit hard in the May 3, 1999, tornado).

The storm produces multiple tornadoes and clips northwest Norman, doing minor damage to the HealthPlex hospital at I-35 and Tecumseh Road, and downing power lines. The tornadoes are "rain wrapped," meaning the storm trackers are unable to see them. The sky, I'm afraid, has that sickly green color of "tornado days." It looks as if someone vomited all over the atmosphere. The storm drops over six inches of rain in south Oklahoma City and Moore, prompting the capital city to issue its first-ever "Flash Flood Emergency." The storm stalls before intensifying and producing a tornado.

Another tornado levels homes in the small town of Blanchard and destroys a motel and mobile-home park in south Oklahoma City, which is inundated with high water. One storm tracker says, "It looks like the entire sky is on the ground, just churning."

The tornado that hit Bridge Creek appears to have been a half-mile wide, and meteorologist David Payne estimates it as an EF3. Numerous tornadoes erupt in western Oklahoma and other storms are now forming in the southwestern part of the state, slowly moving northeast.

Tonight, after the storms lose much of their energy and become more rain, hail, and high-wind producers than anything else, meteorologists tell us we have three more days of potential severe weather to come, with Saturday expected to be the most problematic.

———

May 7: Local news is reporting one fatality related to last evening's storms. A woman drowned when her underground storm shelter flooded. Twenty thousand residents across Oklahoma City and Norman are without power today.

At 4:00 P.M., a line of storms forms just to the west of Oklahoma City and marches north-northeast. David Payne says these storms will move into the metro, bringing us rain and possibly small hail. The tornado threat is, mercifully, low, but David warns that it will be higher tomorrow (Friday), and higher still on Saturday, which, he says, "brings us the highest tornado threat so far this season." He says the largest of yesterday's tornadoes have been rated F2 (south Oklahoma City), F1 (Norman), and F2 or possibly F3 (Bridge Creek). He adds that there were fifteen or so other, smaller tornadoes.

It is windy again today, though not as bad as yesterday. It's also overcast and humid. Heavy rain is falling west of Oklahoma City. I wish we could pack up and leave here for a few days until the weather is sunny and calm again.

———

May 8: At 4:00 p.m., the National Weather Service in Norman issues a tornado warning for Kiowa County in western Oklahoma,

after a firefighter in Hobart spots a twister. The storm that produced the tornado is packing one-hundred-mile-per-hour winds.
Another storm just west of Oklahoma City is now intensifying.
There is rotation with this storm, although our meteorologists are
saying the atmosphere here in central Oklahoma is not as unstable
as it is in the southwestern part of state. Thunder rumbles outside.
The sky has been overcast all day. Temperatures are in the high
seventies and the air is once again thick with humidity. The ground
is saturated from recent rains, so flash flooding is a concern.

Many storms are developing in western Oklahoma, moving
east-northeast. I receive a notice on my phone that all activities
related to Oklahoma City Public Schools are canceled for tonight
and tomorrow. The wind shear with the El Reno storm is now at
fifty miles per hour, and it's bringing a lot of rain with it.

At 4:35 P.M., it seems the storm may have weakened a bit,
but meteorologists are warning us to remain vigilant. A storm
just south of the metro area is moving north, toward Moore and
Oklahoma City, where we don't need any more rain. A flash-flood
warning is in effect.

The first storm passes El Reno and moves northeast, toward
Piedmont and eventually Edmond. Reports are coming in of base-
ball-sized hail in the town of Carnegie in southwestern Oklahoma,
and it seems there is water flowing over Highway 81 in El Reno,
just west of Oklahoma City. The sky over central Oklahoma is dark
and low.

The storm just to our west has now passed Piedmont and is
nearing the western edge of Oklahoma City, while the south storm
is moving north. The two are about to converge on the capital city.

By 4:55 P.M., the three-hour rainfall total for some areas in
western and southwestern Oklahoma is three inches or more.
Ellen left work fifteen minutes ago. I hope she gets home before
the storm arrives.

It's now 5:00 P.M. and David Payne says the circulation has weakened for the storm approaching from the west. Circulation for the storm near Blanchard, however, is increasing, and it's moving toward Norman.

———

May 9: Tornado watches, severe thunderstorm warnings, and flash-flood warnings. Missed my brother's college graduation. Our weather here is terrible. It seems it's dangerous even to go outside.

———

May 16: The atmosphere is primed for yet another tornado outbreak. There's a big tornado this afternoon in southwestern Oklahoma near the Red River, and another in western Oklahoma near Elk City.

———

May 19: Tornadoes are spinning up this afternoon in southwestern Oklahoma as a large and severe storm moves through that part of the state. Another storm has produced several small tornadoes east of Lexington. It's now 4:00 p.m. and a line of severe storms is moving across western Oklahoma toward the capital city. The atmosphere in southern Oklahoma (south of I-40, according to David Payne) is more unstable and conducive to tornadoes than here in Oklahoma City.

———

May 25: Out of town for Memorial Day weekend. When we return, the power is out in our neighborhood from a storm that has just passed through. The streets are still wet, the atmosphere thick and sticky. We wait for thirty minutes or so until the power is restored. Storms over the weekend have increased the rainfall total for the month, making May our wettest month on record according to the Oklahoma Mesonet, whose records go back to 1895. The Mesonet, a world-class network of 120 environmental monitoring stations, featuring at least one in each of Oklahoma's seventy-seven counties, indicates that as of Sunday afternoon (May 24) the state's rainfall total has reached 12.29 inches, which is 8.61 inches above normal. And there's still another week of May remaining with more storms on the way.

Reservoirs across Oklahoma are flooded and closed. Reports have water flowing both through and over the top of the dam at Lake Texoma, which is absolutely inundated by the floods. Lake Altus-Lugert in southwestern Oklahoma has been especially impacted by the five-year drought and was thirty-one feet below normal just a month ago. Reports indicate that it's now only two feet below normal. The lake is coming back up, even as Oklahoma trout fishing is floating away. Floods have blown out the Lower Mountain Fork River.

―――

May 26: More severe weather. More tornadoes. More flooding. A massive, slow-moving storm drops eight inches of rain on northern Logan County, just north of Guthrie. A news reporter places the blame for all this rain on El Niño and warmer waters in the Pacific Ocean, where the evaporation of water into the air feeds into the southern jet stream, which seems to have been stationed over Oklahoma for the past month.

―――

May 27: The sun is shining! It's a beautiful morning!

Warm and humid this afternoon. It feels like summer as I run.

Late this afternoon, at 5:00 P.M., a large tornado is reported in the Texas Panhandle near the Oklahoma border. More severe weather is expected this evening. Storms, if they hold together, will be in the Oklahoma City area around 10:00 or 11:00 P.M. tonight.

―――

May 29: This morning, my barber says he heard that Lake Altus-Lugert is now back to normal levels. There was flooding last night in Lawton, in southwestern Oklahoma, after a slow-moving storm dumped six inches of rain. Flooding has become the real concern across our state. Residents of a neighborhood in southwestern Oklahoma City have abandoned their homes as worry mounts about a lake dam failing. A friend mentioned that earlier this week the dugouts in the baseball diamond near her home were flooded and full of fish. It's Friday and another day (evening) of severe weather is expected before relief arrives in the form of clearing skies and a dry, sunny weather pattern for the first time in a month or more. It can't get here soon enough.

Yesterday morning I noticed an indigo bunting on my back-yard feeder. It was a first-year male with blue head and shoulders, fading into brownish-gray plumage on its wings and back, and a white belly.

At 8:15 A.M. I spot a Mississippi kite flying toward its nesting site along my creek, carrying a foot-long, pencil-sized stick in its beak. Its wing tips make a tapping sound when they strike either end of the stick as the kite flaps its wings. There are a number of kites here in the neighborhood, building nests along the creek. They've blessed us with their graceful presence now for several weeks.

———

May 30: No signs of the rain meteorologists predicted we would receive. Instead, the day is overcast but dry, changing to partly sunny later in the evening. Finally, it seems we have a dry weather pattern ahead, and with only two days to go until June, I'm hopeful that summer weather will be arriving soon.

JUNE

RED-EARED SLIDER

I stopped my car as I was leaving my neighborhood today in order to move a turtle out of the way of traffic. It was a red-eared slider, often called a "pond slider," and of a rather flat constitution compared to a box turtle. Its body was ten inches across. This turtle appeared to have come from one of the neighborhood's ponds, although not recently, for it was perfectly dry. Algae patches were growing on its carapace. I'm told that as long as the shell itself is healthy—this one was—the algae are usually harmless. These green patches may even help turtles blend into their environments.

Red-eared sliders occur naturally in Oklahoma and are native to the Mississippi River valley from Illinois to the Gulf of Mexico. They're found from the Appalachian Mountains in the east to as far west as eastern New Mexico. These turtles are often kept as pets, however, and this had led to their introduction into other areas of the country, as they often escape or are released into the wild. For this reason, they're considered an invasive species. Regardless, and because they're one of Oklahoma's native reptile species, I found no reason to assign any such pejorative designation to this one. I carried it into the woods across the street, away from the constant stream of lumbering automobiles, where it could make itself at home among the trees along the creek.

FRONT-ROW SEAT

Sitting on the back porch of a morning or evening, reading or listening to the sounds of the woods and creek, is one of the summer season's great pleasures, provided we burn a candle or two to deter the stinging, blood-seeking mosquitoes. A pair of Bewick's wrens has built their nest in an open-sided cabinet on our back porch, and this evening as I sat here reading, I heard their nestlings chirping from within this boxy shelter as one of the adults emerged and prepared to fly off in search of food. It hesitated when it saw me and hopped around near the edge of the cabinet, as if contemplating whether to leave its young. A few moments later it disappeared into the recesses of the cabinet, at which point the babies ceased their high-pitched whining and became silent.

The adult wren—the male, I assume—has been busy bringing insects to the nest, especially morning and evening. If I'm on the back porch, it instantly spots me upon its return and will wait nearby, flying back and forth from tree to tree, until we rise from our seats and go into the house. Only then does it approach the nest.

This evening I saw a ten-inch rat snake on the back porch. I scooped it up with a shovel and relocated it to the creek. Just a week ago, I had to perform the same maneuver, only with a very large rat snake. This larger snake struck at the shovel blade several times, at one point latching on. Perhaps sensing the futility of doing so, however, it soon resigned itself to defeat, and to being relocated to the creek as gently as I could wield the shovel. Most years, we see no snakes, although during the drought of 2011 we found several near the house, along with many mice. Sometimes in September, when the nights begin to cool but the long, hot days continue to warm the bricks of our home's exterior, I find one lying along our foundation, attracted by its warmth. Fortunately, so far, none of these serpents have been of a venomous variety, but they're unnerving nevertheless, and during the warmer months I have to watch where I step.

I suppose this is one of the setbacks of living near a creek, of having nature—even the cold, slithering variety—for neighbors, but it's a compromise we've learned to accept. More troubling is finding the aforementioned rat snakes near the house during spring, when the birds are nesting. I understand that some snakes will return each year to the specific trees where they've pilfered bird nests in the past, which makes me wonder about these along my creek. I'm leery of rat snakes. Once, while visiting the Tishomingo National Wildlife Refuge in south-central Oklahoma, I came upon an old shed whose open interior featured, high on each wall, a continuous series of swallow nests, a dense concentration of mud-daubed tenements safe from all but those vertically inclined serpents. The frenetically feeding birds were flying about in great numbers, and I dreaded their return to the nests because one of them wouldn't be so lucky. A rat snake had scaled the wall and was waiting in ambush at one of these nests. I might have relocated this intruder but for the futility of such a view. For I knew he'd be back.

SIGHT FEEDER

The eastern bluebird is a sight feeder. I see one perched on a limb outside my office window and watching the ground below, turning its head this way and that, tilting it just so, and the next moment swooping down to the ground and, missing its mark, circling around for another go. The bird hovers in the air only inches above the grass, until its prey—a moth—is located. At this point, the bluebird collects its prize and makes a blue beeline toward its nest or another tree in which to dine.

At 5:20 P.M. on the evening of June 6, I watched another bluebird, an adult male, resplendent in its cobalt dinner jacket, doing exactly this. Not far away, on the same limb, was a juvenile bluebird with blue wings and tail, and barred chest and shoulders, mimicking its father. A few moments later, two other young bluebirds appeared on the same limb. Together they studied the grassy area beneath them. In contrast to the juvenile titmice, which appear almost identical to their parents but for their slightly smaller stature, the young bluebirds were about the same size as their father. Watching them poised on the ash limb outside my window, I was reminded of miniature hawks perched in a tree or on a power line, their sharp eyes taking in everything occurring beneath their small section of sky.

THRASHER

An adult brown thrasher pecks at the sunflower seeds I just set out, hammering like a woodpecker and then running a morsel over to one of its two fledglings waiting nearby. They're nearly identical to the adult in both color and size, and unlike the California thrasher I've seen so often in the Golden State, darting across desert trails and into the chaparral, our brown thrashers aren't particularly bashful and are of no mind to hide. One of the young birds ruffles its feathers and appears to vibrate as if announcing its hunger. The adult teases the youngster, now offering the seed, keeping it just out of reach of its snappy beak, now pulling it away. Finally, when the fledgling moves far enough, the adult concedes the seed, evidently satisfied its charge has demonstrated the requisite authority or sufficient effort with which to feed. As for the young bird, perhaps it gleaned from this exercise the lesson that there is no such thing as a meal for free.

GRASSLAND MELODY

Visiting the open grasslands and meadows here in central Oklahoma this time of year is to treat one's ears to the field sparrow's melodious song, so sweet and clear. It begins with a few sharp,

high-pitched notes that build upon one another and quickly converge into a gorgeous trilling blend, regaling us for a moment
before trailing off and dissipating as if carried away by the wind.
Interludes are mercifully brief, during which time these graceful
melodies echo through one's mind until the field sparrow's song,
an audible treasure in kind, is then repeated, over and over again.

AN EVENING WALK

The first stop tonight is our neighborhood swimming pool, which
as a rule is usually deserted of swimmers of an evening. I rest my
elbows on the fence and glass the meadow overlooking the creek. I
sight a cloud of gnats swarming over the waterway and then spot a
flicker preening in a tree. A cardinal alights nearby and then flies
away a few seconds later, apparently unimpressed with the flicker's
vainglorious need.

Moments later, two green herons fly by over the creek, vigorously pumping their wings and calling to mind the great blue
heron I spotted on my morning walk not far from here, flying low
and slow toward the same section of creek where I see these birds
year after year.

Swallows are scrawling their names in cursive in the airspace
above the meadow and generally putting on quite a show. Now an
eastern kingbird appears, in the very same tree in which I've spied
them in previous years, its subdued plumage in sharp contrast to
the yellow belly and chest of the western kingbird I watched for
several minutes the other day only a short distance from here. A
moment later it dives from the tree and swoops toward the ground
to capture a fluttering moth. The kingbird appears to lose sight of
its prey, however, and now at a loss for anything else to capture and
eat, hovers only inches above the grass, trying to spot the elusive
insect with the frenetic wings. Sighting it once more, it swoops in
again. Somehow, the moth escapes clean.

In the park, the wildflowers are delightful this time of year. The purple coneflowers are only just beginning to wither and droop after being in full bloom for the past few weeks. Along with these I spot purple prairie clover, *Gaillardia* (Indian blanket), and bull thistle, that prickly and free-seeding weed with the fringy hat of pink. Best of all are those scattered patches of plains coreopsis, expectant yellow faces oriented toward the west, leaning forward like a theater full of children riveted to their seats, awaiting the G-rated picture show newly released.

Passing over the creek, I look down and see a snapping turtle, its knobby carapace fifteen inches across. It is lying in a bottleneck, facing upstream and waiting for the current to deliver a meal to its maw. Even from my elevated position on the bridge, I can't help but notice the size of this turtle's head. It's as large as a softball, with terribly efficient and powerful jaws.

When I return home, an eastern phoebe is perched on a tree limb in my backyard. It flies to the ground, snaps up some insect, and returns to its perch in a maneuver often called "hawking." Because it feeds on airborne insects, this bird tends to winter in areas where streams and ponds remain unfrozen during the dormant season, thus allowing for regular hatches of aquatic mayflies, midges, mosquitoes, and others. George Sutton notes in his book *Fifty Common Birds of Oklahoma* that the phoebe often winters in Oklahoma, and though considered an eastern species, it nests throughout the state.

JULY

MAGNOLIA

Way back in May when the magnolia trees were flowering, blooming buttercups blessed these otherwise monochrome monarchs shading our windows and crowding our eaves with pert petals that floated on thick green leaves like whipped cream on coffee.

Now, as these blossoms wither and fall away, one of the magnolia's crackly leaves, having burned and browned, clatters through the branches and flutters to the ground where it lies until stirred by the wind, and then, careening through the breeze, skids onto the street where it skims over the pavement like a skipping stone, following the wind's current to some distant yard to await its fate with the lawn-cutting machine.

MOCKINGBIRD

Everywhere I turn it seems there's a mockingbird. Stalking the creek banks in crepuscular clothes. Fluttering from tree to tree like a low-flying bomber on patrol. Harassing the blue jays. Escorting an occasional crow out of established airspace. And always singing, around the clock, day and night, cycling through a ceaseless repertoire of notes, hosting its own call-and-response solos, easily entertained, easily triggered to strafe an odd grackle strutting into the yard. A few dive-bomb runs and the intruder retreats to some other ground less contested. And then all through the evening and long past dark, the mockingbird calls, from the redbud tree out front, from the hedgerows over in the park, from the top of a lone pine across the street, regaling us in its melodic panoply, reminding us that if we have time to breathe, we have time to sing.

KITES

Mississippi kites are patrolling the skies, surveying the neighborhood with high-altitude eyes. Two months ago, I saw one of the first kites of the year. It had a long strand of cellophane in its beak as it slipped into the trees to construct a home. Now these raptors are everywhere, from morning until evening, circling the skies with wings spread wide, riding the spiraling thermals higher and higher, indifferent to the biting sunshine, whirling and wheeling, the very picture of freedom, now adjusting their broad wings, folding them in just so until the birds, seen from below, resemble diving *M*s in the sky.

A kite alights on a bare treetop. It looks left. It looks right. It slowly scans the surrounding airspace. When its radar eyes detect insect intruders, the kite, the short-takeoff artist, is instantly aloft, now cutting in behind the bug whose invisible movements I can trace only through the kite's shadow-swift reactions: the tucking, the diving, the swift midair turnabouts. Then the kite plucks the insect from the sky and returns to its treetop perch where it devours its meal, bite after bite until the kite, its hunger as yet unappeased, scans the sky once more, turning its head left, then right, then left again, head spinning on its bone socket nearly a full 180 degrees so that the kite is looking almost directly behind it, as an owl might, and then slowly back to the right, seemingly indifferent to the frenetic mockingbird calling from an adjacent treetop, cycling through its mimicking repertoire that includes cardinal and crow, kingbird, bluebird, and now a blue jay—*jeer, jeer, jeer!*—and then back to the cardinal's sweet song while the Mississippi kite, its fiery eyes locking on to some other infiltrating insect, opens its wings and falls away to meet it.

ANTS

A fire ant scrambles along the edge of the swimming pool in dusk's fading light. Its frenetic movements catch my eye, and when I look closer I see why. The fire ant is hoisting a carpenter ant twice its own size, as if the latter had just scored a winning goal and helped claim some ant championship, or as if the larger carpenter ant had, only a moment ago, correctly assembled the letters of some esoteric, polysyllabic term and, in doing so, claimed the first-ever spelling-bee title for a small country school that no one, beyond the ants themselves, has ever known. But alas, victory has eluded the listless and seemingly unresponsive carpenter, which the fire ant struggles to secure as it races along the poolside to the flaming horde now relieving their industrious comrade of his prize.

ROADRUNNER

A roadrunner appears in my backyard, possibly the same road-runner from yesterday, from last week, ducking its head and running, then pausing, then running again, and now pausing once more, tilting its gaze to the left, to the right, its bright brown eyes scanning the lawn for something I can't see. Now it lowers its head and tail and rushes forward like a fullback, muscular thighs churning and carrying the bird across my gridiron yard. When the roadrunner runs, when it lowers its head and tail and runs, it forms a right angle, like a carpenter's square, or like three bases in a baseball diamond. When the roadrunner runs, when it lowers its head and tail and runs, one could, if one found such things entertaining, draw a line from its head to tail and it would make a perfect forty-five-degree angle. If it were a roof, the bird's broad back would shed rain falling from the sky, keeping the occupants warm inside. Now the roadrunner runs into my flowerbed and leaps onto the edge of our birdbath, which, as we have not anticipated a thirsty roadrunner, we've left dry. Undaunted, the bird hops to the opposite side of the bath and raises the feathers on top of its head, an iridescent comb glinting in the sunlight as it surveys its surroundings, looking first to the left and then to the right, soon spotting its own reflection in the window. The roadrunner leans in for a better view and then offers the window a glimpse of its profile before looking back, returning its gaze to the familiar bird in the glass. It repeats this process, quicker this time. And then again. Is this a game? Now the roadrunner hops to the other side of the birdbath, leaps to the ground, and races to the far corner of the yard where it seizes a small snake. The bird then flips the snake up into the air and, before the serpent lands, snatches it once again and rushes into the trees.

CLOUDS

Clouds at sunrise, dominating the horizon like a distant mountain range, snowcapped and serene and, with each passing minute, fleeting, like water splashed on the sidewalk in the middle of the day. Clouds at sunrise in the sleepy morning sky, at one moment looming, menacing, and the next retreating to another clime and place, a different season. Clouds at sunrise losing their low-altitude disguise as the orange orb ascends, melting the snowcapped mirage, liquidating the barrage of steamy runoff funneling, pooling, dissipating into nothing as the distant haze is replaced at last with blazing rays and a brilliant blue sky, a reminder that around here it never snows in summer, it seldom rains in July.

OAK

A lone post oak standing at attention beside a busy city street, its authority unchallenged by the ranks of less imposing trees behind it. This tree wears its rank in concentric internal rings, which tell the story of drought and flood, of famine and feast, of discouraged settlers who took but a few swings with the axe before taking their leave, of deferring developers who built their road to accommodate the tree, circumventing its muscular trunk, its broad branches and thick green leaves, which, in shape, suggest a cross. Was it these leaves for which this strange transitional forest was named? Or was it the barrier this arboreal band represents? The Cross Timbers. When the first European explorers came through here in the early nineteenth century, this tree, this lone post oak, was already two hundred years old and a veteran, undoubtedly, of many heat waves and droughts and spring storms, its roots anchored to the sandstone substrate beneath it, roots that help this lone post oak, and others like it, to endure, persist, and survive winter's ice sheaths, summer's searing heat. A charter member of these Cross Timbers, a living natural-history museum whose gnarled branches and bark-covered knobs tell of centuries of buffalo neighbors and, more recently, the marauding mobs of bulldozers that have claimed so many of its comrades, this lone post oak remains resolute in the oxygen it offers, graceful in the shade it provides, generous in the treetop perch on which our Mississippi kites alight, and as suited as ever to survive the harsh climate of the southern plains, to live and breathe and thrive.

AUGUST

DIVE-BOMBERS

While jogging through our neighborhood this afternoon, my wife was dive-bombed by a Mississippi kite. I was envious. For the past two years, I've been hoping this would happen to me. It's not that I wish to provoke the kites into attacking, nor do I suspect the kites would actually attack, but rather bluff. But I want to experience this so I can better understand the protective instinct of this elegant bird. So far, though, and despite jogging nearly every chance I get, I've not had the privilege. Maybe they sense my benevolence, or, seeing me struggling to run, they sense that I'm no threat to their nests and perhaps take pity on me.

She said—and this really made me envious—she was eye level with the kite, that she could see right into its eyes, which were focused on her. It came within five feet of her before swooping up and away, at which point Ellen began waving her arms in the air to ward off the bird. When she next looked up, the kite had disappeared. In describing this kite, she mentioned its "spotted chest," which told me it was a juvenile, probably a second-year kite assisting its parents with nesting—in this case, security—duties. I'm not sure many second-year kites establish nests of their own. Perhaps some do. I'm inclined to believe many more enter into an apprenticeship whereby they learn the finer points of nidification and parenting before going off alone.

Mississippi kites are famous for this behavior. It's their natural, protective instinct. Unfortunately, it gets a lot of them into trouble, especially on golf courses, which are attractive to nesting kites for their isolated stands of tall trees surrounded by open grasslands in the form of manicured fairways. This is the type of open-range habitat Mississippi kites prefer, especially for nesting. Also, it's one reason why Oklahoma, with its scattered Cross Timbers forests in the eastern and central part of the state, and isolated cottonwoods and willows and elms and shin oaks in the west, is so attractive to these birds. In most cases, these trees are surrounded by vast open spaces that provide good hunting for the kites while also allowing them to sight, and defend their nest from, potential predators—even perceived predators, such as golf-club-wielding humans. Golfers frequently experience the kite's defensive instinct, although many falsely perceive that the bird is out to attack. As a result, the golfer swings, injuring the unfortunate kite, which can now no longer protect and defend and feed its young. It's a tragic situation and one that's becoming more and more common. I'm not sure what the answer is. Protective buffer zones, perhaps, although this would require reconfiguring most golf courses, at least those here on the southern plains and elsewhere in the kite's nesting range. On the other hand, this certainly presents an opportunity for conservation-minded golf-course designers and municipalities, many of which are now beginning to realize the myriad benefits—economic, social, biologic, ecologic, and aesthetic—of urban forests and as a result are working to better manage and conserve these important areas. Perhaps one day we'll realize that golf courses, like urban forests, like community gardens and public parks, can serve more than a single purpose.

FOOD CHAIN

It's very hot and humid of late, as is typical for the southern plains states in August. The wrens call of a morning, while the cicadas creak throughout the day. You spot them lying in the grass as you mow the lawn. Lately, I've noticed many small brown frogs hopping about in the yard and along the foundation of my home. I suspect they are plains leopard frogs, which are common visitors around here at this time of year. They're eating insects, which I welcome, but these small frogs also attract snakes, which attract the roadrunner that eats the snakes. The sight of these large cuckoos running across the lawn certainly appeals to salivating bobcats and coyotes, which I find fascinating and which I'm constantly seeking to celebrate through close observation and field notes. Whenever I see one, I try to grab my binoculars before it disappears into the forest or the mercifully undeveloped meadow of field grasses across the creek, to which developers, like the deer in my area, seem to gravitate.

Like the coyote, the roadrunner has thrived and managed even to extend its range over the past century, in part because of its varied diet. It's omnivorous, the roadrunner, much like the coyote, eating nearly anything it can catch and swallow. This includes grasshoppers, crickets, caterpillars, moths, scorpions, tarantulas, centipedes, and millipedes, as well as larger prey such as lizards, skinks, frogs, horned toads, snakes, small birds and mammals, and even sumac berries and other plant food. Roadrunners were once persecuted for their diet, which many believed included a disproportionately high ratio of quail eggs and nestlings. Consequently, some states even paid bounties for this bird's destruction until government studies eventually debunked this myth.

As one might expect for a bird with such a diverse diet, the roadrunner's methods for obtaining its food are equally varied, clever, and refined. In her book *The Real Roadrunner*, Martha Anne Maxon notes that these foraging techniques include "wing-flashing," whereby the roadrunner pauses to extend its wings in order to flush insects or lizards, a behavior I've observed in mockingbirds;

following herds of feeding deer to capture insects stirred from their hiding places; trailing farmers whose plows expose grubs and other edibles; and even ambushing its prey. "The roadrunner may wait, catlike, in ambush outside animal holes or near bird feeders until unsuspecting prey appears," Maxon writes.

Perhaps most intriguing, however, is its ability to kill and consume snakes, especially rattlesnakes. This, writes Maxon, "is one of the greatest tests of the fighting skill and mettle of the roadrunner," and it's made possible through the bird's lightning-quick reflexes, powerful bill, and shrewd technique, which Maxon describes:

> The bird first slowly circles the snake sideways with tail fanned and tipped toward the snake, then jabs at the snake's head with lightning speed. The bird will often flash its wings rapidly, revealing white patches, as it circles the snake. . . . When the snake strikes back the faster-moving roadrunner leaps out of reach of the strike, then begins jabbing at the head again. . . . The final kill is made by repeated jabs to the snake's head. Sometimes a pair will work together in a team attack, with both circling the snake until one gets an opportunity to jab at the snake's head.

This same speed and quickness that have made the roadrunner famous in American popular culture also help it evade its own predators, such as hawks, which Maxon says sometimes dive at roadrunners in open areas. "No eyewitness accounts of a predator killing or disabling an adult roadrunner have been reported," she writes. "In all reported predator attacks on an adult roadrunner, it has escaped by making swift maneuvers or seeking cover."

ECLIPSE

Today's solar eclipse is the first one I can remember since 1979, when I was a kid. I recall my friend Tracy Jones having the opportunity to observe the eclipse through some special viewing gadget the school had procured, and afterward him drawing on the chalkboard a picture of the crescent-shaped sun to show our class what he'd seen and what everyone was then talking about. Today I glimpsed the sun but once, and that was accidental and for only a fraction of a second, as I was painting the eaves of my house and chanced to glance up for some reason. Rather, I paid much more attention to the shadows of tree leaves, which appeared as a cloud of individual crescents on my back porch. They reminded me of small bats in shape, although they changed quickly, becoming thicker and in a matter of minutes seemingly ovate.

This afternoon the ambient lighting dimmed but did not go out. Here in central Oklahoma we were treated to only a 90 percent eclipse. Perhaps this wasn't the full eclipse they had up in the Midwest and over in the Mississippi River valley, but it was close enough. The sun was still bright, but less so than usual. It felt like being outdoors on a full-moon night.

Gradually, the leaf reflections on my back porch began to resemble a school of small fish assembled tightly just beneath the surface of the sea. When the leaves shimmered in the breeze, the fish became swimmers on the water's surface, ripples on the open ocean and its vast blue sheen. Like any pelagic fish, they didn't remain on the surface for long. As the light gradually brightened, the fish glimmered and veered, finally descending into the gin-clear depths where with the passage of the eclipse they disappeared to some future year.

On my run this evening I saw two yearling deer, still with spots on their lean bodies. They paused and stared as I jogged by, huffing for breath, grasping for grace in my mildly suffering state. Though wide-eyed and alert, they did not bound away, even when I said hello. These deer obviously had not been hunted, and it was so refreshing to see how wild animals respond to our presence under such circumstances. Yet perhaps their confidence is ultimately to their detriment. A few days ago, I spotted two young raccoons run over on the road not far from my neighborhood. I am still thinking about them today, troubled at the tragedy and such a waste of two beautiful animals. There must be some way to prevent these needless killings, but I don't have the answer. I wish I did. The best solution I've yet seen is that utilized on Florida interstates, which are bounded on both sides by a continuous fence. This certainly helps, but it's not perfect. After all, the state's miles of forested and grassy medians serve as viable microhabitats in their own right for a variety of species, which even here must contend with constant traffic, day and night. If I could invent something, anything at all, it would be an inconspicuous and innocuous device designed to deter wildlife from our busy roadways, thus safeguarding life, theirs and our own.

SOUNDS OF SUMMER

Cicadas humming full tilt through the long afternoons, and well into the nights. Blowing wind, rattling the leaves in our deciduous trees, and soughing, almost whispering, through the pines. The steady cry of a young Mississippi kite, calling from its nest as its parents hunt high in the sky. Unseen birds whistling from the woods. These birds discerned only from their calling, the cardinal, titmouse, chickadee, and starling. A squirrel scolding some unseen intruder. A single tree frog creaking throughout the night, even as dawn approaches, even as the others fall silent. A soloist violin-playing cricket. A Bewick's wren calling from a cedar thicket. The low, steady rumbling of a thunderstorm drawing off into the distance, leaving a peaceful hush over a landscape glistening and wet.

SEPTEMBER

SHOULDER SEASON

For the second consecutive year, Ellen and I are forced to cancel our trip to Jacksonville (Florida) on account of a hurricane. This year, the storm that's impeding our travel plans is particularly large, strong, and slow moving. Downtown Jacksonville is flooded. Senator Marco Rubio commented to the media recently that folks no longer have hurricane parties like we did for Hurricane Hugo in North Carolina back in 1989. The reason is that large, destructive storms are becoming more common and the smaller hurricanes less so.

The weather here in Oklahoma is beautiful. Skies are sunny, winds calm, and temperatures pleasantly warm, in the eighties. And yet despite the weather, for all practical purposes summer is over. The kids are back in school. People are talking—when they're not talking about hurricanes—about football, the upcoming Halloween, and autumn's gold and orange leaves. Winter is coming and soon Florida will seem again like the place to be.

I walked at the park this evening and noticed a mockingbird stalking the sidewalk edges, pausing every two seconds to open its wings as if trying to flush reluctant insects out of the grass. I've seen them do this of a summer evening in the little meadow behind our swimming pool, but to what effect I couldn't say. A siren sounded toward the north, inciting the park's coyotes into an impromptu howling performance that lasted a half minute or more.

Big bur-oak acorns litter the neighborhood sidewalks and creek edges. They're so large they resemble small pineapples. Squirrels are staying busy by burying these acorns in my backyard. When they sit in a tree and eat them, you can hear their chewing and gnawing from quite a distance.

No sight of any kite now since returning from Michigan three weeks ago. There weren't as many kites here this year as last, and those that were here appear to have vanished overnight, unlike last year when we had wave after wave of the birds stopping in the neighborhood on their migrations south. Interestingly, these migrating kites would stay days with us and travel overnight. When they arrived, they would often select the same trees that our resident (nesting) kites had vacated only days or weeks earlier, which speaks to the qualities kites seek in their nesting and roosting sites.

Only a few trees along the creek have webworms. None of my trees do, which is a blessing after the infestation we had last year. It was the worst webworm season I've yet seen.

I watched a wren on my back porch yesterday. It explored every nook, including the cabinet where a pair of these birds raised a brood last spring, and a couple of decorative boats my wife has set out, which are filled with seashells. The bird appeared on the gunwale of one of these boats and then went below for a look around before emerging. When it did, it must have seen me, for it stood up straight and even stretched on its toes as if seeking a better view. Then it flew away.

An eastern phoebe has been frequenting my backyard in recent weeks. It lands on an ash limb, where it scans for insects. This bird can look directly behind itself as it searches, spinning its head a full 180 degrees. Though it lands on a limb near the feeder, the phoebe wants no part of the sunflower seeds.

A red-tailed hawk soars back and forth over the creek behind my house, screeching. As this occurs, a barred owl hoots several times from the forest. I notice a hatch of caddis flies coming off the creek. If there were any trout in these waters, now would be the time to tie on a size-fourteen elk-hair imitation. The bluegill, I've noticed, usually aren't as selective, which is why I elect to leave them be. We're on the cusp of fall, after all, and the fish have made it through the hottest days of summer. They deserve a rest, and an idle buffer, before winter.

At the park, there's an orange ribbon remaining on one of the elm trees. It was placed here last summer, indicating the presence of a kite nest so walkers and joggers could perhaps veer around this sensitive area, or at least take heed. The tree is located near the road and the nest was situated quite low in the canopy, such that I could almost touch it, which I found surprising, indeed.

Not far away, I came upon a fig tree. The fruit was red and smelled sweet. There were lots of mockingbirds about. They ignored a fuzzy caterpillar inching its way across the sidewalk, evidently preferring to save their appetites for these figs. Meanwhile, an eastern phoebe sat on a power line nearby, contentedly repeating its own name, *fee-bee, fee-bee.*

Later, I noticed a pecan tree. The husks were splitting open and the nuts already beginning to fall. They were early this year. Usually this happens in late October and November. I blame the rains we had in August, which fell this year in a most uncharacteristic abundance. Not far away was an Osage orange tree with its crop of rough-skinned fruit scattered on the ground beneath it. This, the bois d'arc, is the tree many Southern Plains tribes used in the construction of their bows, and the tree that, as Josiah Gregg notes in his 1844 book, *Commerce of the Prairies,* the French so named for this very reason. He adds that the wood is "of a beautiful light orange color and, though coarse, is susceptible of polish, and is much used by wagon-makers and millwrights."

OCTOBER

AUTUMN

Out in the lakes, bass are leaving their deep summer slumber and invading tranquil shallows where, like green bullies, they crash hapless schools of shad and minnows. Morning's crisp, nose-biting air reminds us summer is on the train now, departing from the station and heading southbound with bouquets of ornamental warblers. In the forest, sweetgum leaves smolder in preparation for the season's impending conflagration, and winter's frost. Here at home, my son exchanges T-shirt and shorts for cardboard jeans and woolly sweater, its scratchy sleeves tickling arms and skin now prickling at cranky teachers' voices, after-hours arithmetic, and those strangely fabricated student lunches, served up in assembly-line fashion right there in front of him.

The mockingbird in my backyard has sung so sweetly all afternoon as the wind has gusted, as the phoebe has hunted from the ash tree, as the chickadees and cardinals and titmice have shared the seed in the feeder, as the squirrels have busied themselves with the seed scratched onto the ground beneath it, as my dogs have lazily and happily napped around the house, and as I've struggled, along with everyone else, to make sense of the day's horrific news from Las Vegas.

How is it that nature is so purposeful, so reasonable and respectful, while humanity is at times so callous and arbitrary and ugly? Animals seem to regard one another with more respect than we humans, who so often tell ourselves we're the higher, more intelligent, more sophisticated creatures. I think we're wrong on this much more frequently than we'd like to believe, and today's news reminds me why.

There's a gentle rain falling. Low thunder rumbles in the distance. Skies are dark and gloomy. And yet the mockingbird in my backyard seems determined to make the most of the stage it's been given. It is singing steadily, emphatically, jubilantly. Celebrate the day, for tomorrow is not guaranteed, it seems to say.

SCISSORTAIL

Air temperature reaches into the sixties today, which is thirty degrees lower than yesterday. It's been windy of late. Yesterday's breeze was out of the south; today's wind blows from the north. I'm sure the cold front is pushing more birds southward.

Today at the park, I saw two scissor-tailed flycatchers, Oklahoma's elegant state bird, each perched on its own section of power line and each facing into the north breeze just as fish orient toward the current. They were looking out over the spacious field before them, perhaps pondering their winter migration, or simply seeking dinner. I was surprised to see the birds here this late in the year, although when I checked my journal I saw that I made the same observation about them last year, on October 12 (today is the fifteenth). I then checked my *Date Guide to the Occurrences of Birds in Oklahoma*, 2014 edition, and found that the scissortail has been documented here as late as November 18 across most of the state. Interestingly, the 1986 edition of this guide lists the date as November 2, which perhaps reflects some minor variability in the birds' habits year to year, decade to decade. But it also suggests the importance of getting more people involved in bird-watching to increase the amount of quality data available to science for the determination of such matters. It may be that scissortails were here for many days after November 2, back in the early and mid-1980s, but that no one recorded or observed them at this advanced date until much later. And what of the change, if any, in annual temperatures between the 1986 and 2014 editions of this guide—a period of twenty-eight years? Might global warming ("climate change") encourage scissor-tailed flycatchers to remain longer here in Oklahoma before migrating to the tropics? I would think so, and on the surface at least, the 2014 *Date Guide* would seem to support this.

Regardless, there is to my eyes no more iconic symbol of Oklahoma than the scissor-tailed flycatcher perched on a barbed-wire fence or rural power line, presiding over its territory, watching the world go by. Though its beauty and grace are some of its most endearing traits, we can admire this bird also for its heart. The scissor-tailed flycatcher is closely related to kingbirds, and like kingbirds it vigorously defends its nesting territory against trespassers small and large. As aviators, they are aces. One sunny summer day I watched a scissortail porpoising through the warm air as if without a care in the world. It attempted to land on a pear seedling and, evidently finding this perch too flimsy or bare, immediately fluttered away to another. Then, while it was still in the air, the bird's mate appeared and up into the sky they went at a surprisingly high rate of speed. Seconds later they descended toward the earth, swooping down in a blur and making a couple of quick loops and a sudden turn before alighting in an oak tree nearby. Watching them, I had to smile, for at rest these svelte birds with their long tail feathers give little indication of their acrobatic design.

Later, on the opposite side of the park from the scissortails, I noticed deer tracks on the paved walking trail. Like mud tattoos, they were crisp and full, probably laid down last night, revealing the deer's easy and unhurried gait as it emerged from the cedar and sumac thicket nearby. I followed the tracks off the walkway and onto a well-used game trail that cut through another thicket and led a short distance away to a clearing, where the deer could bed down out of the wind, or browse the oaks and elms along the margins.

For the past several afternoons I've heard the high-pitched trilling of a tree frog in the forest along my creek. It strikes up about four o'clock, while the skies are still bright. There is but one frog creaking this evening. We're expecting the season's first freeze tonight and the birds are crowding the feeder. I hear a flock of starlings across the creek, and I hope they remain there. Once they discover the seed in your feeders, they become a nuisance, these purveyors of greed.

There has been a skunk in the backyard for the past several nights. I know this because, while I don't detect even a hint of its scent, when I let the dogs out in the morning their sniffing betrays this weasel's overnight visit. It too has been frequenting the bird feeder. Though the skunk can't reach the feeder itself, it has been cleaning up whatever debris the birds have scratched out onto the ground, eating its fill. Tonight, as I went to let the dogs out before bed, our skunk was on duty and though the dogs chased it out of the yard, they trotted back to the house reeking of that putrid, pungent odor that skunks deal at will.

My dentist tells me she has a skunk that enters her backyard through a hole in the fence, and it eats the sunflower seeds she sets out for the birds. I didn't realize these seeds were so appealing to skunks. Perhaps mine was attracted to the suet cake hanging from one of my redbud trees. Some animal continues to scale the tree, dislodge the feeder, and drag it into the woods, where it makes short work of the greasy suet cake even though it can't open the wire-mesh cage containing it. After all, this suet is redolent of peanut butter and berries. Though it is no doubt appealing to the skunk, I'm certain the suet-cake caper is the work of a raccoon, opossum, or even a gray fox, which is capable of climbing trees and which I've sighted in our backyard in winters past.

I tried the oatmeal shampoo we keep on a bench near the washing machine. This is all we had on hand. It helped, but it didn't erase the skunk stench. The next day I bathed the dogs in tomato juice. This helped a bit more, but it didn't last. Two days later I could still smell skunk. As it turned out, the solution was time, a couple of weeks of frequent ablutions, and even a trip to the groomer before the odor subsided.

NOVEMBER

NEW ARRIVALS

I returned from Louisiana to find that winter had arrived in Oklahoma, despite the date on the calendar. Temperatures were in the eighties in central Louisiana but are hovering only in the forties with a gusty north wind here in Oklahoma. The meteorologists are calling for rain tonight and a chance of snow.

The cotton had just been harvested in Texas and Louisiana. It was stacked in large plastic-covered rectangular bales at the edges of the white-flecked fields. Here in central Oklahoma, our cotton is ready for picking. This fluffy fiber was once considered "king" of southern crops, but the boll weevil and falling prices served to undermine it over time. It's still grown around here, especially in southern and southwestern Oklahoma, and to me there's nothing that calls to mind the image of the American South quite like a field of cotton in bloom. My grandmother used to tell me stories of picking cotton as a child on her father's farm. This was in the early years of the twentieth century, before mechanization, when the crop was harvested by hand, stuffed into long burlap sacks, and weighed at day's end. The sharp ends of the cotton bolls would prick her fingers as she reached for the white fibers, drawing blood and, she said, producing tiny warts on her fingertips. She got rid of them, though, by collecting one small pebble for each wart, spitting on the pebble, and placing these rocks into a box, which she wrapped up to look like a gift or a package meant for delivery.

Then, on a full-moon night, she dropped this package at a four-way intersection and recited this chant: *Wish I may, wish I might, have this wish I wish tonight.* Shortly thereafter, the warts were gone.

The autumn foliage in our area is at its peak now, in the second week of November. We're not seeing much color from our oaks, but rather from our ornamental sugar maples with their brilliant orange and yellow canopies. Some of the red maples are beginning to shed their rainbow halos, and their leaves now blanket the ground beneath these trees in thick mats of red, orange, and pink.

After I cleaned up the yard last week, a single day of strong winds ripped most of the clinging leaves from the oaks and walnuts and elms along our creek, blanketing my backyard in an almost solid layer of additional work. It is gloomy and damp today, though not especially cold. After reading Lafcadio Hearn's descriptions of Japanese flowers and gardens and their muted and graceful colors, and the Japanese talent for assembling flower sprays consisting of not a full bouquet but a single and complete limb, and after studying Clementine Hunter's colorful paintings of her cheerful and vibrant zinnias, I am eagerly awaiting spring.

This evening the sun appeared and the birds came with it—a pair of cardinals, some chickadees, mourning doves, Bewick's wrens, a red-bellied woodpecker, blue jay, and Swainson's thrush, which I spotted hunting on the ground in the far corner of my backyard, near the forest. It's a migrator here but we haven't had weather cold enough to urge it on. This one likely came from the north ahead of the recent cold front. In any case, it is late in the season for this bird to be hanging around. My 2014 *Date Guide to the Occurrences of Birds in Oklahoma* indicates September 30 is the latest date the Swainson's has been recorded here. "Climate change," I hear ringing in my ears.

An hour later I spot the thrush in a small tree near the creek. When the dogs and I venture into the backyard, the bird does not fly away but contents itself with the food it seeks. My *Date Guide* from 1986 lists September 11–30 as the departure-date range for the Swainson's thrush here in Oklahoma, adding that this bird is a rare fall migrant to the state.

Regardless, it is here quite late in the year, and I delight in observing this bird for the next several days, along with many yellow-rumped warblers that have arrived in an overnight wave and now flit through the trees. This latter bird is a couple of inches smaller than the thrush, with distinctive yellow patches on the rump and flanks, but with a similar mottled coloration on the breast. Like the thrush, it has a thin bill. Unlike the thrush, however, the yellow-rumped warbler occupies a space high in the tree canopy, near the crown, whereas the Swainson's thrush orients toward the ground and is seldom found far from it. In this, they are like different species of fish occupying separate areas of the water column—or people, some of whom prefer the visibility and myriad distractions of city life, while others find meaning and purpose in living close to the earth, in the country.

THANKSGIVING

Spent a lovely Thanksgiving Day at my brother Matt's place, near Stratford, Oklahoma, a small town known for its peaches but that could be, and maybe should be, known just as well for its pecans. The trees are everywhere here. Matt has three separate groves of these pecans, one of which is located along a creek where he recently placed a game camera to survey the deer and other wildlife using the creek's riparian corridor. So far, he has captured video of a gray fox, a bobcat, and interestingly, a couple of river otters. The section of creek I observed, near the pecan grove, was narrow and shallow, but there must be deeper pools and wider stretches of stream elsewhere on the creek, water capable of supporting these animals and the fish on which they feed.

Matt said his pecan crop was hampered by an unusually rainy August, which he believes caused so many of his pecans to fall prematurely. The nuts were stuck in the shucks and the kernels were undeveloped. This is something I've heard repeated recently in Texas and Louisiana, and elsewhere in southern Oklahoma. A few of Matt's trees still clung to their ill-fated pecan crop. I picked a few of these pecans, which lacked the heft of nuts containing the welcome treat of solid, healthy kernels. Cracking the shells revealed the void that should have been filled with sweet pecan meats.

We watched a pair of nuthatches, flying one by one to a feeder on a pecan tree near Matt's house. The birds would land on the side of the tree opposite us and move around to the side with the feeder, which they would approach from behind. Even this, the feeder, they used as cover, keeping it between them and us. At a glance, as it moves along the tree trunk, the nuthatch resembles a downy woodpecker, at least to my eyes. A moment later, however, its true identity is revealed.

Temperatures today reached into the midseventies, which isn't unusual for an Oklahoma Thanksgiving. Winds were calm and the sky clear and bright. Autumn has been dry this year, and very pleasant.

Back at home this evening I heard splashing sounds coming from the creek. It was a large animal, a coyote, I assumed. Actually, it was three deer, two does and a yearling. They moved up the creek bank and began browsing on the grasses at the edge of the meadow, despite my neighbor's barking dog, and despite the sight of me standing on my back porch, watching these peaceful animals through field glasses. These deer are accustomed to living close to people, to barking dogs, and at times to the stentorian noise of traffic out on the main roadway leading toward town. This doesn't mean they're indifferent to these various stimuli; it's just that they're accustomed to hearing and seeing them. So long as they keep tabs on our location, they feel content to step into the meadow of an evening and browse. Watching them, I was reminded of the doe I came upon many years ago while out hunting for, ironically, deer. I was using a tactic called "still hunting," slipping through the woods with rifle in hand, pausing every few steps to look and listen. In this type of hunting there is always more pausing and listening than moving, or ideally, there should be. I was working my way into a south wind and after some time I heard the yapping of dogs headed my way. I paused and waited while the cacophony of excited canids approached my position, just off a well-used game trail. Presently, I noticed movement and along came a couple of deer, an adult doe and her yearling. They were bounding through the forest at what seemed top speed, and strangely, unexplainably, when they reached a point in the trail opposite me, they turned in my direction and leaped into a thicket. There they stood not twenty feet from me, frozen and motionless, their long necks twisted around behind them, looking back toward the trail. A few moments later—it couldn't have been more than a half minute at most—a pack of three coyotes came into view, racing along the trail in pursuit of the deer, yapping and barking in excitement. They ran right past the two deer watching them, past me, also watching them, and continued down the trail alternately sniffing at the ground and yapping as they ran at high speed. Through all this I didn't move a muscle. I stood there watching the two deer as their ears followed the gradually fading frenzy of the coyotes until they were out of range, at which point the deer turned and looked directly at me. Again, I didn't move. I was dressed in camouflage hunting gear. I was even downwind of the deer. And yet they sensed my presence. Even more surprising was that they appeared to understand that I posed them no harm, despite the hunting rifle in my hands and the deer tag in my pocket. But watching the deer veer off the trail and elude the hungry coyotes, I became their ally rather than another predator. I cheered for them as they narrowly avoided this danger, knowing they needn't worry. I wasn't so much a hunter as an observer, a witness, a kindred spirit even. I was grateful just to be there and to watch these two deer escape the jaws of danger. A moment later the doe turned her head and gently bounded away, the yearling right behind her, disappearing through the trees.

I recall them this evening as I watch these three deer across the creek, trying to make a living in a world that seems to crowd them, to threaten them, a bit more every year. I am thankful that they still have this riparian corridor, the creek and meadows and the surrounding remnants of Cross Timbers forest in which to live out their lives. And so do I. It's been a beautiful day.

DECEMBER

CHRISTMAS TREE

Now that the leaves have fallen from the oaks and elms and walnut trees behind our home, we've lost our summer screen of privacy, our shelter from the dizzying world across the creek and out beyond the road. On the other hand, this seasonal exposure is only temporary, and it permits us to see into the interior of our little woodlot as if peering into its soul. Limbs and branches are scattered about, cluttering the understory. One of my trees is dead but still standing. Most, however, appear to have weathered the long growing season very well and have arrived on winter's doorstep in great shape. A few are fading and tired, and yet they remain upright and functional. Every year we seem to lose a tree to high winds or old age, and I'm compelled to remove these fallen timbers even though they're organic and would eventually provide some benefit to the soil were I to leave them. But as steward of this vital strip of trees—vital for the birds and squirrels and occasional deer, if not for me—I strive to keep it neat and uncluttered because this is the way I found it when my family moved into our home twelve years ago. Managing our miniature forest, this precious microhabitat, has become in some sense a welcome tradition, like the holidays we celebrate at this time every year.

Today, among the dead and dormant wood, I spot a new sign of life: a young cedar. I hadn't noticed it previously. It's growing at the edge of the creek bank. The little tree is not yet three feet tall.

Its fledgling limbs are thin and sparse, but somehow it appears full in the way that all evergreens appear dense and full when viewed at a distance. It is a splash of green on the gray slate surrounding it, a reminder, or perhaps a promise, of the spring yet to come. It's a sign of life amid its dormant deciduous counterparts, an oddity of sorts, a breath of fresh air, this tree that stands apart from the others. Looking at it reminds me of Christmas, for not only is the season upon us, but this little cedar would make a splendid holiday tree. I won't cut it down, though. It's much too beneficial for the creek bank, and the stream itself, and, by extension, my backyard. And though its oily boughs could fuel the flames of trouble in some parched year, considering its diminutive size and the season, I cling to the idea of reprieve. Not only this, but as it grows the little cedar will help fill in those gaps in the surrounding foliage, enhancing my green shelter screen come summer, come spring, when noisy automobiles roar up and down the nearby roads.

Once, many years ago, my family visited a tree farm after my wife had won a voucher good for a free Christmas tree. Upon our arrival, we were given a bow saw and pointed toward an emerging forest of green. After some consideration we selected a spruce, or a Scotch pine. Exactly which it was I can no longer recall. It was about five feet in height, an adolescent as it were, on its way to greater things. It was a beautiful tree of a perfectly proportionate conical shape, and although grown expressly for this purpose, much too pretty to cut down. I told myself that we were upholding—and introducing my young son to—an old and cherished American holiday tradition. But afterward it felt like a frivolous thing to do. We secured the tree to the top of the car and carried it home—someone honked and waved at us along the way, evidently impressed that we were doing our part, in steadily falling snow, no less, to keep this quintessential holiday tradition alive—where we placed it on a stand and draped its boughs with ornaments and bows. It served us well for a few weeks, until the big day had passed. Now sated on Christmas music and holiday cheer, we turned our attention away from the tree and toward the imminent New Year.

By now the tree was drying out and it dropped a trail of needles on our tile floor as we hauled it to the curb, a green and brown trail that crunched beneath our feet. Some days later the city collected it and carried the tree away, ultimately converting it to mulch with which to blanket someone's flowerbed, or using it to fill a void along some stream bank, a void created perhaps by the absence of trees. Anything but to smooth the scar we created when we cut it down. A little piece of me must have gone away with the tree because the evanescent indulgence we'd allowed ourselves in adhering to this old tradition troubled me for days, for weeks, for a long, long time. Repeatedly, that old Emily Dickinson poem cycled through my mind: "Nature—sometimes sears a Sapling / Sometimes—scalps a Tree— / Her Green People recollect it / When they do not die—." Unlike the tree, my scar wasn't so visible. But it was there, and I carry it to this day.

I resolved to never cut down another tree for Christmas, a holiday for which it seems more appropriate to celebrate rather than appropriate—and ultimately terminate—our landscapes' natural gifts, especially a young tree with decades or more yet to live. And birds yet to shelter and nourish. And land yet to stabilize and preserve and defend from erosion. And streams yet to protect from runoff. And fish yet to cover in cool shadow. And air, the very air we breathe, yet to freshen with its invigorating evergreen scent.

As I pick up the scattered debris from my woodlot I take care to ensure that no errant branches or limbs impinge upon the little cedar standing nearby at perfect attention, like a toy soldier keeping watch over the creek its boughs will eventually shade, I hope for many Christmases yet to come.

PART II
RED DIRT COUNTRY

HOLDING PATTERN

The flight from Dallas to Oklahoma City is only thirty minutes. That's less time than it takes me to run four or five miles (obviously, I'm a sorry runner, but I enjoy it nevertheless). One can't listen to John Coltrane's *Giant Steps*, the full album, in that brief span of time. In fact, I can't even drive from the Will Rogers World Airport, in southwestern Oklahoma City, to my home on the metro area's far northern fringes, in thirty minutes. Which is why I didn't leave the airport when my wife, Ellen, phoned to say her plane hadn't departed Dallas as scheduled. For to do so would inevitably have resulted in my phone ringing just as I pulled the car into the driveway, and Ellen telling me the plane had finally departed and that she'd see me in a mere half hour. *Don't be late!*

Already, I'd been in the car too long, running errands, taking my son to a late lunch and dropping him off at the theater, sitting in traffic through yet another construction zone—why do these arterial obstructions always appear where *I* want to drive? Stuck in the airport parking lot, I realized what I needed was to get out of the car and stretch my legs. Exercise. After all, it was one of those beautiful spring days that we see occasionally here on the southern plains— eighty degrees with only a light breeze and the vast Oklahoma sky a brilliant, daydream-inducing blue with not a cloud in sight.

Reasoning that I had time to walk a lap around a nearby park, I pointed the car's front bumper north and put the terminal and its fields of concrete, its signage canopy, in my rearview mirror. Exiting onto Airport Road, I soon found myself facing an immense seam of cars. Congestion never used to be an issue here. Oklahoma City's growth over the past twenty years has changed this, however.

Unable to turn back, I had no choice but to integrate into this smog-producing throng and inch my way out to the highway. My knees and back ached. I wanted desperately to get out of the car for a few minutes, to surround myself with trees and grass and fresh air. Relief was painfully slow in coming, however, and by the time I reached the park twenty-five minutes had passed. Which meant that I didn't have time to walk. Which meant that I needed to turn the car around and head immediately for the airport. After all, Ellen's plane would soon be landing. And there was all that traffic.

Don't be late!

Somehow, I made it back to Will Rogers World Airport in only fifteen minutes. I found a parking space at the edge of a small field where I could at least see something natural and green, something other than concrete, metal, and glass. I rolled the windows down and turned on the radio, changing the channel several times until I found a station whose announcer wasn't jabbering about politics. As I listened to talk of the ongoing National Basketball Association playoffs, and whether the Thunder should double-team the Spurs' seemingly unstoppable scoring machine named LaMarcus Aldridge, I spent the next thirty minutes mentally tracking Ellen's plane from the runway in Dallas to the Oklahoma City tarmac. Then my phone buzzed with a text message.

Mechanical trouble, the message read. *Back at the gate! Getting off the plane!*

Oh, joy, I thought. More waiting! All I could muster in response was a digital frown.

I wanted to escape from all this monotony. But how? Of the two main roads leading away from the airport, one was inundated with traffic and the other under construction. Where could I go until Ellen's plane arrived? What could I do? I imagined myself a fish that had swum through a narrow funnel and found itself trapped, its freedom suddenly and inexplicably restricted. Even if I had been able to leave, home was forty-five minutes away. My thoughts began to spiral downward. My pulse raced. My chest tightened. And when even the sports channel descended into the abyss of political chatter, I felt like punching my radio. Instead, I saved my knuckles and simply turned it off.

It was midafternoon on a midweek day in early May, and despite the hubbub out on the roads beyond the airfield, the parking area where I was sitting was quiet and languorous. With the radio off, the din of traffic silenced by distance, it wasn't long before I heard the first bird singing. It was a house finch, a male, perched atop a nearby pine tree. Its cheerful, exuberant tune seemed offered in celebration of the beautiful afternoon. Now I began noticing other birds. The field to my right appeared to have been plowed recently, and atop the miniature mountain range of cultivated earth in the near distance was a barn swallow. Presently it jetted off, vigorously pumping its wings, flying low to the ground as it headed toward a fence to my left. Once it reached the fence, the swallow turned back and returned to its perch on the furrow of overturned earth, where it rested a moment before repeating the process. This little bird looked so jubilant, as if thrilled, as if energized by the sudden understanding that it could fly, swiftly and gracefully, which it did again and again.

I heard mourning doves cooing somewhere nearby, and minutes later a couple of the birds came into view, sailing over my car and alighting, one on a light post and another on a low concrete wall. Soon they fluttered to the ground, looking like angels as they descended, and began canvassing the parking lot for food.

By this point in late spring, the mockingbirds had been singing for several weeks. I'd enjoyed listening to them around my house and all over the city, everywhere I went. There were a couple of them here at the airport, whistling from their perches on the fence, regaling me with their enthusiasm and considerable musical talents.

Now a black grackle came strutting up to the fence and the mockingbirds went to work, alternately dive-bombing the grackle with swift, swooping runs that seemed to perplex the larger bird, who was being strafed now from one side, now from the other. This persisted only a short time before the grackle, perhaps realizing that holding this territory wasn't worth the cost, soon retreated, taking cover beneath a parked car.

I was delighted at my new and unexpected discovery, and I felt some surprise that even an airport could support such a vivacious community of birds, and probably other wildlife. How was it that I'd never noticed? At some point I realized my pulse had slowed and the tightening in my chest had eased. I'd even forgotten about my aching back and knees, my urge to get out of the car.

Occasionally, a large silver or beige bird would appear suddenly in the distance, its nose angled sharply upward, its landing gear retracting as whooshing jet engines pushed it away from the earth. Now sparrows were darting back and forth over the parking lot like fighter jets, agile and fearless as they banked and descended on some morsel of food.

Sitting in the narrow parking space between the open field and the distant airport terminal, I was reminded that a parked car makes a great bird blind. And with the radio off, insulated as I was from the congested roadways in the distance, beyond the airfield, I could actually hear what was happening around me, the sounds of nature, even a small slice of it, going about its business, making the most of a pleasant spring day regardless of the many obstructions that had sprung up around it on every side, and reminding me that despite what the text messages said, despite the DELAYED signal flashing on my mind's list of scheduled arrivals, things were right on time. Soon, summer's heat would envelop the southern plains, and the fearless flyers and ebullient singers all around me would restrict their activities to very early or very late in the day, hours when they'd likely go unobserved to all except those savvy enough to tune in to nature's frequency and adhere to her schedule. *Don't be late!*

FIRES

It's May 2014 in Oklahoma and much of the state is under a governor-issued burn ban. And until we receive some rain, some relief from the drought that's persisted like a virus for the past three years—lying dormant during the brief, damp period of spring, only to rage through the long summer months when the lack of moisture is most acute, the parched landscape most vulnerable—charcoal grilling, campfires, and most types of outdoor burning are prohibited.

This is nothing to trifle with, for even something as seemingly innocuous as steering your car off the pavement, where a hot muffler, say, could come in contact with kindling-dry vegetation, or running a metal-bladed edger along the seams of your thirsty lawn could spark a blaze that, with any encouragement from the wind, would burn for days. And while dropping cigarette butts on the ground is a deplorable habit anytime, under these conditions it could cost you a thousand dollars, a year in prison, and potentially much more. As outlined in the governor's May 5, 2014, ban on outdoor burning, "in addition to the penalties prescribed in the law for violations of the outdoor burning ban, operators may also be liable for damages caused by a fire, and for the cost of suppressing such fire."

This executive proclamation also includes fire-related guidelines for activities such as road construction; welding, cutting, and grinding; oilfield and landfill work—interestingly, "gas vents and flares associated with the extraction of oil and gas or the refining of oil and gas (or other manufacturing processes or landfill operations) are generally considered exempt from the ban as long as the top of the vent pipe is raised well above the surrounding vegetation"; the clearing of storm and land debris; campfires and outdoor cooking; state fire schools and associated fire training; and, yes, fireworks.

All this is good and well. But these precautions can only reduce, not eliminate, the likelihood of becoming a victim of the current drought and the area's tinderbox conditions. A spark, some fuel, and a breeze to fan the flames are all it takes to transform these gently rolling hills and their grassy carpet into a charred moonscape in a matter of minutes.

As an Oklahoma native, I'm accustomed to droughts every several years. It's part of the natural cycle here on the southern plains, along with, unfortunately, tornadoes and floods and ice storms. And yet there comes a certain point in any drought, especially one as severe as this, where it seems my neighbors and I are strangely like chemists or sabotage artists working to disrupt the fire triangles of heat, fuel, and oxygen that naturally converge all around us. But even as we undermine these triads by limiting the heat component, for example, through our burn bans, a potential disaster is never more than a single oversight away, for an errant spark, malicious or otherwise, can produce a potentially life-threatening fire. Especially when temperatures hover at the century mark for weeks at a time. Especially when the incessant winds feel like a convection oven blowing across your face. And especially when one of your neighbors deems himself King of the Barbecue Machine, and thus immune to the no-fire orders causing culinary frustration for the rest of us. And because we've built lives here with our families and homes, we don't take off our lab coats until the rain arrives to relieve us of our duties. That's because reverse-engineering our way to a solution to this drought, to the severe wildfire risk, is not an option.

With the gusting wind and the blistering sun that each day bakes my lawn to a crisp, protecting my home from a wildfire seems a tall order, especially considering the scattered trees and wooden skeletons in the housing development taking shape between my own neighborhood and the busy roadway a half mile to the south. So, with rapt attention, I sit and watch the local news reports, waiting for word that the wind is abating, the fire risk decreasing for a few hours, long enough that I can get some sleep until the flag-snapping breezes return again tomorrow.

And then it happens.

Outside my window, a plume of dark smoke is spilling into the sky to the east. Somewhere, somehow, the three components have found each other. The triangle has succeeded. Ignition has been achieved. We have fire and, suddenly, reason to worry.

———

The Land Run of 1889, which opened the Unassigned Lands of Indian Territory—what is today part of the state of Oklahoma—for settlement, may be remembered for exactly what it was: one of the most amazing feats of the nineteenth century, and one of the most egregious. At noon on April 22, thousands of settlers, many from the East, lured west to the plains by the promise of free land, rushed into the territory on horseback, in covered wagons, by train, by bicycle, even on foot, to claim a piece of the nearly two million acres the U.S. government had recently allocated for disposal. By nightfall, the Oklahoma landscape was transformed as new towns had sprung to life along the Santa Fe Railway.

Shortly thereafter, an article appearing in *Harper's Weekly*, written by William Willard Howard, who'd witnessed the Land Run, described it this way:

In some respects the recent settlement of Oklahoma was the most remarkable thing of the present century. Unlike Rome, the city of Guthrie was built in a day. To be strictly accurate in the matter, it might be said that it was built in an afternoon. At twelve o'clock on Monday, April 22d, the resident population of Guthrie was nothing; before sundown it was at least ten thousand. In that time streets had been laid out, town lots staked off, and steps taken toward the formation of a municipal government. At twilight the campfires of ten thousand people gleamed on the grassy slopes of the Cimarron Valley, where, the night before, the coyote, the gray wolf, and the deer had roamed undisturbed. Never before in the history of the West has so large a number of people been concentrated in one place in so short a time. To the conservative Eastern man, who is wont to see cities grow by decades, the settlement of Guthrie was magical beyond belief; to the quick-acting resident of the West, it was merely a particularly lively town-site speculation.

This is to say nothing of the Native American tribes, which had been forcibly removed from their homelands in the southeastern United States and relocated to Indian Territory during the 1830s. To the Chickasaws and Choctaws and Cherokees and Creeks and Seminoles, who'd been forced to vacate millions of acres in Georgia, Florida, Mississippi, and Alabama, the Land Run of 1889 and subsequent land runs were the result of yet another broken promise by the U.S. government, which had assured the Indians this land would be theirs forever.

Though it doesn't excuse the government's betrayal of the Indian tribes, it's easy to see why settlers wanted to come to Oklahoma, where there were vast tracts of unoccupied land, oceans of prairie for grazing, abundant sunshine, and water. Washington Irving wrote about the area in his book *A Tour on the Prairies* (1835), based on his 1832 journey through Indian Territory. He describes being in awe of the alluvial soil and lush trees, the grassy plains and peaceful wooded groves his party encountered along the Arkansas, Canadian, and Verdigris Rivers. He also mentions the plentiful wildlife, especially buffalo (American bison), which remained a mainstay for the Native Americans who lived here until the animals' decimation by white "hunters" a half century later.

In addition to experiencing the territory that would one day become Oklahoma, long before European settlement, at a time when the land was still unfenced, unadulterated, and practically unexplored by outsiders, Irving witnessed smoke from Native American fires, which they used to control wildlife, their primary food source. The Indians burned forests and prairie not only to enrich habitat for the animals, but also to drive buffalo and other species during hunts. They saw fire as a tool and they used it to survive.

Similarly, on his journey into Indian Territory in 1819, Thomas Nuttall observed smoke from these fires and commented on it in his *Journal of Travels into the Arkansas Territory, during the Year 1819* (1821):

> Among the more remarkable features of the autumnal season in this country, is the aspect of the atmosphere, which in all directions appears so filled with smoke, as often to render an object obscure at the distance of 100 yards. The southwest winds at this season are often remarkably hazy, but here the effect is greatly augmented by the burning of the surrounding prairies, annually practiced . . . for the benefit of the hunt, as the ground is thus cleared of a heavy crop of withered grass, prepared

for an early vegetation in the succeeding spring, and also assisted in its growth by the stimulating effects of the alkaline ashes.

Fire has played a major role in shaping the North American landscape through the ages. Ignited by lightning, wildfires swept across the land, eliminating forest undergrowth and fertilizing the soil. But as the country was settled, the suppression of wildfires began as families sought to protect their homes and other property.

Soon, fire—physical fire, the heat-producing process of combustion—was all but excluded from the natural cycle, supplanted by our burning desire to construct synthetic worlds that we could control. As new cities and towns appeared across the continent, fire was viewed more as a threat to our nascent civilization than as the ecologically sound, beneficial process it had always been.

My great-grandfather Howard Jackson was seven years old at the time of the Land Run in 1889. His family came to Oklahoma from Texas and eventually claimed 160 acres in the run. He would spend the rest of his life on this land, farming, raising children, and struggling to survive the Oklahoma weather.

A century later, on the eve of his one-hundredth birthday, in 1982, a newspaper reporter interviewed Howard, inquiring about his long life and his memories of Oklahoma's early years, which dated to that April day in 1889 when his family had gathered with all the other families along the sandy banks of the South Canadian River, waiting for the cavalry officer on the white horse to fire his gun and set that line of humanity into motion, fording the river and fanning out across the plains in search of new lives.

I have a copy of the newspaper article that resulted from this interview and count it among my most prized possessions, for my grandfather describes in fascinating detail the challenges his family faced in holding on to their claim in the days when self-sufficiency was the rule. He mentions floods, tornadoes, outlaws who tried to wrest away the land through gunfire, and a certain blizzard that piled up so much snow on his family's dugout shelter that the roof collapsed.

He also mentions raging wildfires that could be contained "only with the help of every able-bodied man in the area." Even then, in the late nineteenth century, wildfires were being suppressed across the southern plains and elsewhere as the wild American frontier was gradually tamed.

In succeeding decades, as modern civilization has grown, as our cities and suburbs have expanded, so too has our aversion to fire. Ironically, however, fire suppression has had exactly the opposite effect from what we intended. While it reduced the number of fires in the short term, ultimately it contributed, and continues to contribute, to an increased risk of wildfires today.

———

The plume of smoke has grown taller, darker. The fire might be two miles away, or twenty. I can't tell. I go out on my back porch for a better look and hear sirens wailing in the distance. Moments later I'm back inside, watching television coverage of the blaze. A local news helicopter broadcasts aerial views of the conflagration, which has engulfed a field and is sweeping quickly to the north, pushed along by the wind and leaving a smoldering black blanket in its wake. The chopper circles the scene from above, bringing us views of residents scrambling to get horses out of barns, belongings out of homes, automobiles out of driveways and garages. The area is shrouded in smoke. Now the fire finds a grove of cedar trees, and their oily boughs explode into flames. Hot embers, riding the wind, jump a road and eventually drop into other fields, igniting them, expanding the blaze and inundating the firefighters struggling to control it.

I get a text message from my wife, then a friend. Am I watching the news? Of course. Everyone's watching the news because everyone knows that his or her home could be next.

Am I going to do anything? What can I do but sit and wait, and prepare to jump in the car and hit the road at a moment's notice? It's a terrible feeling watching a wildfire; you feel helpless, the way you do as you track a tornado that's twisting its way toward your neighborhood. You want to leave and put the danger behind you. And yet you can't tear yourself away from your home. This is your life; everything in the world you own is right here. Are you going to relinquish it to the weather, or to potential looters? Or are you going to stay and fight for it? Of course I'll stay and protect what's mine for as long as I can. But I know, eventually, there'll come a point where I'll have to cut and run. In the face of an advancing wildfire, an ordinary garden hose isn't much use.

I look around the house, wondering what I'll take with me if I have to flee. My family's photo albums? Clothes? My wife's Hummel collection?

Outside, the sirens are growing louder.

———

While originally intended to encourage the responsible use of matches, the ethical disposal of cigarette butts, and the careful management of campfires, Smokey Bear's "only you can prevent forest fires" message, which was broadcasted widely throughout the second half of the twentieth century, inadvertently portrayed all fires as detrimental to the land. The image of a shovel-toting bear clad in a forest ranger's hat—the same flat-brimmed hat that he grew to define, and that became known as the "Smokey"—depicted foresters as being averse to any kind of blaze whatsoever. Yet our foresters would later strive to reeducate a public that was, and still is, misinformed about fire. And as research began revealing fire's benefits to an ecosystem, Smokey Bear was compelled to update his message, as well. Today he reminds us that we're the only ones who can prevent wildfires.

But fire not only benefits an ecosystem; it's an essential component. Scientists tell us that altered fire regimes have contributed to the imperilment of the shortleaf pine forest, for example, which once covered much of the eastern half of the United States, from New Jersey to Florida and west to Oklahoma. Over the past thirty years, this forest has lost half its original range. Despite this, it still stretches across twenty-two states, where it has a tremendous cultural, ecological, and economic value, especially for wildlife, human recreation, and water quality. This was a primary driver behind the formation of the Shortleaf Pine Initiative, a consortium of stakeholders with representatives from the U.S. Fish and Wildlife Service, National Bobwhite Conservation Initiative, University of Tennessee, American Forest Foundation, National Fish and Wildlife Foundation, The Nature Conservancy, and other organizations working together to help restore the shortleaf pine forest ecosystem. Naturally, fire figures prominently into these efforts. According to the U.S. Forest Service's 2006 report *Shortleaf Pine Restoration and Ecology in the Ozarks: Proceedings of a Symposium*, frequent burning, in one- to four-year intervals, aids in the regeneration of these trees, though more infrequent fire (intervals of eight to fifteen years) "promotes survival and recruitment into the overstory." Researchers believe this eight- to fifteen-year fire cycle is crucial for the shortleaf pine's ability to prosper, especially in areas with abundant hardwood trees, which compete for the same soil nutrients and sunlight.

Scientists point out that fire is an ecosystem driver, facilitating processes such as nutrient and water cycling, and working in conjunction with herbivory (plant regeneration through animal consumption) and climate in the natural restoration of many ecosystems. Fire, they say, is mandatory for the health of the prairies, shrublands, and forests throughout most of the world. They also point out that while land managers today have many tools at their disposal, there is no substitute for fire.

Without periodic burning, the forest understory grows congested with brush and nonnative vegetation, which competes with native plants for soil nutrients. Periodic burns eliminate this clutter, which is itself a primary wildfire fuel, while contributing organic elements to the soil. This encourages growth of native plant species and helps return a forest to its original, natural state of productivity and diversity.

Periodic burning also contributes to the early green-up of plants and grasses. This is significant because the vegetation is substantially higher in nutrients, like crude protein, which benefit wildlife and domestic grazers like cattle and sheep. It's also more palatable.

Some plants, such as the shortleaf pine, actually require fire to complete their life cycle. Young trees grow quickly after the tops have been "fire killed," while mature trees, by virtue of their thick bark, are protected from all but the most intense blazes.

It seems that our society is only beginning to understand what many Native American cultures have known about fire for ages. Accordingly, we're seeing an increase in the use of prescribed burning as a land-management practice, which reflects a proportional improvement in public education about fire's benefits to an ecosystem. But while these benefits are well documented, the practice of prescribed burning, often called "controlled burning," remains controversial because of the risks it carries, especially when performed close to human habitations.

———

A fire truck and police car enter my neighborhood, stopping in front of a house just down the street, their lights flashing *emergency!* The firefighters jump off the truck and one races up to the house while the others work to connect a hose and assemble their gear. There is no smoke coming from the home; I wonder whether the fire could be indoors. Is anyone inside? Behind me, the black plume of smoke has grown into a giant cloud that hangs over much of the eastern horizon above the advancing wildfire. I can't see the flames from here, but I smell the smoke. A few minutes later, the firefighter emerges from the house down the street and says something to the others. Everyone seems to relax. I walk down the sidewalk and inquire of a neighbor, who tells me it was a false alarm. "Fireworks," she says. "The kids were shooting them off in the backyard."

Smoke, but thankfully, no fire.

––––––

Scientists tell us that today's larger, more destructive wildfires have unintended consequences even for those ecosystems that evolved through periodic burning. Years of fire suppression have led to such a buildup of fuel that today's fires burn hotter and more intensely than ever, killing even mature trees. This is changing the landscape in some areas. Old-growth oak stands, for example, which have been around for hundreds of years, are being reduced to ashes in some blazes. These trees, such as those found in the Cross Timbers of central and eastern Oklahoma, existed long before Washington Irving visited the southern plains, and many of them escaped the axe and saw simply because they were situated in areas deemed undesirable for farming, or they were too gnarled and twisted to serve as lumber for building. But these grand old trees, which have endured hundreds of years of droughts and heat waves and ice storms, don't stand a chance against today's most intense conflagrations.

Perhaps the most apparent example of fire suppression on the southern plains is the rapidly expanding presence of eastern redcedar trees across our grasslands, which, ironically, increases the fire hazard to human dwellings.

Not surprisingly, many landowners strive to remove the pro-
lific redcedars from their property by cutting them out, or by burning. I've participated in a couple of controlled burns, and on both
occasions eastern redcedars were the landowner's primary target.

Using a device called a drip torch, I spent several days as part
of a ragtag burn crew, canvassing fields and forests and dropping
flaming balls of diesel fuel at the base of the trees. Once I saw
how quickly their oily boughs converted a spark into a raging blaze,
and the ease with which the wind took their burning embers and
scattered them, I understood the hazard they pose to humans.
Though accumulated brush and woody debris is certainly a viable
fuel source for wildfire, redcedar trees are something else entirely.

These redcedars were front and center in April 2018 as another
megafire torched western Oklahoma. At the time, the area was
experiencing what scientists were calling "historic" fire conditions because of an ongoing drought categorized in some areas
as "extreme" and in others as "exceptional," an exceedingly low
relative humidity, air temperatures approaching ninety degrees,
and incessantly strong winds blowing into the state from Colorado
and New Mexico. Less than two weeks after its initial flare-up on
April 12, the Rhea Fire, which began in Dewey County, Oklahoma,
before expanding into nearby Blaine, Custer, and Woodward Counties, had burned more than 285,000 acres, killed two people and
thousands of cattle, and torched dozens of homes. As of April 23,
and despite the rain that had fallen the previous weekend, InciWeb,
the Incident Information System, reported the fire only 74 percent
contained. Smoldering hot spots posed a continuing threat, as did
areas of unburned vegetation. According to InciWeb, these fuels
included tall grasses, brush, and "red cedar."

Recently, my neighbor Keith told me of a friend who'd been
in western Oklahoma on a turkey hunt during the early stages of
the Rhea Fire. It seems this man, Keith's friend, split up from the

others in his party to hunt alone. I'm told he didn't know the land, nor did he realize the winds were pushing the wildfire toward him. Later, however, when he discovered the immense fire raging his way, he recognized at once that he couldn't outrun it. Wondering what to do, he noticed a stock tank nearby, the sort of aluminum pool that writer Edward Abbey once lauded as a "thing of joy to man and beast" and that is still a fixture across rural areas here in the near Southwest. In this part of the country where it can be so hot and dry, these stock tanks and the windmills that accompany them are like Great Plains oases, isolated sources of water that help sustain life. From a distance, they cut a rustic and perhaps quaint silhouette against the distant horizon and wide blue sky. These windmill-and-stock-tank watering stations call to mind farm ponds fringed in wispy willows, or a cottonwood-lined riverbank, their spinning fans and thin metal vanes suggesting shimmering leaves on a windy summer day. There is something incredibly soothing in the purring sounds of a rickety windmill fan spinning in a warm plains breeze, just as it has done for decades or perhaps the better part of a century. Very often, there's nothing other than birdsong or the lonesome howling of a coyote, or the very wind itself, to impede one's enjoyment of these pastoral pleasantries. Yet however picturesque or serene, out here these water-producing implements are vital fixtures indeed. The wind blows the fan, engaging gears that operate a pump designed to draw water up from deep underground. This pooled water provides what, at certain times of year, may be the only reliable source of hydration for miles around.

As the wildfire raged, Keith's friend raced to the tank, jumped inside, and submerged himself. Then, with the forty-mile-per-hour winds blowing the fire toward him, he stepped out, dripping wet, and lay down on the ground in the lee of the tank, on the side away from the advancing flames. Moments later the fire raced by overhead and raged down the hill, a living, breathing wall of heat, now moving away from him. Though it rushed by in an instant, the blaze burned him severely.

For those who've never been around such conflagrations, it's difficult to understand just how much heat a large fire produces. You can feel its sting even from a distance you might deem "safe." A "megafire" amplifies this burning reality even higher.

At the time I heard about this, western Oklahoma was still burning from the Rhea Fire. So was Keith's friend, who was in the hospital, awaiting surgeries and skin grafts and an uncertain future.

For many years Keith served as our neighborhood's groundskeeper, work that involved everything from sprinkler repair to fence painting to tree planting and trimming. He told me of clearing some of the neighborhood's common areas of their red-cedar trees several years earlier and having to field questions and complaints from residents who wondered why he was cutting them down. He said they were adamant he should let them be, until he explained the redcedars' combustibility and the hazard they posed as wildfire fuel. So informed, he said, they began to agree: "Let's take out these cedar trees!"

———

Once, as a child, with the help of my brother and a neighborhood friend, I built a fire in my backyard. I don't recall what possessed me to believe this was in any way a good idea; I do, however, remember thinking it was exciting. And it was, for the fire began as a small blaze, warm and companionable, but grew increasingly larger, hotter, and more raucous with each cedar bough we fed into the flames. Soon it was really churning, and we stood back and watched the flames licking at the sky, wondering how much bigger it would get, wondering whether we should put it out. Then my parents saw us through the patio door, and I knew I was in for it.

They were still yelling at us as we shoveled dirt onto the flames and tamped the fire out. Afterward, my father lit me up with his leather belt and sent me to my room.

———

Despite the necessity of fire in many ecosystems and our efforts to better understand its importance to the landscape, fire suppression remains a problem across much of the country. One reason is the stigma surrounding it. As humans continue to alter the land, fire becomes more and more undesirable because of the threat it poses to our communities. But we can only delay the inevitable; we can't prevent it indefinitely. And when wildfires do occur, the effects of suppression manifest themselves in the form of larger, more destructive fires, which we hear about every year, not only in Oklahoma but across the American West. A case in point: California, which, given decades of fire suppression, overdevelopment, and an insidious and ongoing drought, saw more than ninety-two thousand acres burned from January 1 to September 20, 2014, according to the California Department of Forestry and Fire Protection (CAL FIRE). But even this figure pales in comparison to more recent statistics. In 2017, more than nine thousand wildfires tore through the Golden State, burning more than one million acres of land, destroying more than ten thousand structures, and killing forty-six people. This was a year that saw fires erupt throughout the state, from the Oregon border in the north to San Diego in the south, and east into the Sierra Nevada. The Thomas Fire, first reported in early December 2017, which raged for weeks, prompting mandatory evacuations in Ventura and Santa Barbara Counties before finally being contained, burned more than 280,000 acres. According to the *Washington Post*, it's the largest fire ever recorded in California. The *Post* also reports that most of California's largest wildfires have occurred within the past thirty years, and that five of the most destructive, including the Thomas Fire, burned in 2017.

Concerned—a concern that rightly or wrongly stems from being overstimulated by almost continuous media coverage of natural disasters such as wildfires—about the fire that might happen, that could happen, I've considered removing from behind my own house some of the trees and other vegetation that currently serves as a natural buffer between my backyard and the adjoining creek. While this would certainly reduce—it can't eliminate it altogether, can it?—the risk to my home, removing this vegetation would also have a detrimental impact on the creek, as it would encourage erosion, which would degrade water quality and the structure of the stream bank. And by eliminating, or even thinning, this lush riparian zone, I'd be destroying vital habitat for the many species of wildlife that make their home here. I know this, which is why I'll never do it, even though we see the same type of destruction and adverse environmental impacts whenever raw land is cleared for commercial or residential development.

In Southern California, however, officials aren't taking any chances. After the Canyon Fire 2 raged through parts of Orange County in October 2017, torching more than nine thousand acres along with homes and other structures, and in light of such a severe fire season statewide, the county vowed to step up its fire-prevention efforts going forward. And it is. Goats are now being used to clear large swaths of dry brush from an increasing number of communities, such as Anaheim. The city's fire department believes they're perfect for the job and points to their ability to access dense vegetation along steep hillsides where humans might have difficulty working. Others say goats operate more quickly than humans, and they don't complain. Speaking to a reporter, the man responsible for this fire-prevention task force explained that a single goat eats roughly ten pounds of potential kindling daily, which, for a herd of two hundred, equates to approximately a ton of dry, brittle vegetation removed from the parched Anaheim Hills landscape each day.

The location and placement of housing developments in such proximity to the natural world is a paradox that's replicated all across the nation and, increasingly, the world. We're building ourselves out of a healthy environment, not only by adding concrete, wood, glass, and plastic structures, but also by eliminating vital processes like fire from the ecosystem. As humans, we seek to manipulate and reshape and control the world we live in under the assumption that it's ours, when in fact we're only visitors here, just like the fish and birds and other wildlife. But whenever Mother Nature reasserts her authority, with a wildfire, for example, we're reminded there are consequences for altering the landscape with our buildings and roadways.

According to *Forbes* magazine, in the United States alone, we need to construct 1.5 million new houses each year just to accommodate population growth, satisfy the demand for vacation homes, and counter the demolition of old dwellings. While most of these homes are built in urban areas rather than in rural or wilderness settings where wildfires may pose a greater risk, they nevertheless reflect society's expanding footprint and our own ambitions as humans. And herein lies what is perhaps the crux of the problem: nature's landscapes evolved with the *presence* of fire, while the synthetic worlds we create thrive in the *absence* of it.

So who wins? Nature does, of course. Fire has always played a part in shaping the continent, and it'll continue to do so in the future. What is unclear, however, is whether we'll decide to work with nature or maintain our collective apathy going forward. For our own future and that of our planet, I hope it's the former.

———

One of the greatest short stories ever written, in my opinion, is Jack London's "To Build a Fire." Here we have a tale of that most fundamental human dilemma—the human-versus-nature struggle to survive. Interestingly, and not insignificantly, fire is at the very heart of this story, for if the man with "no imagination" can master his situation and build a fire to dry out his wet boots and feet, he'll survive, at least long enough to continue his trek through the frigid Yukon. If not, he'll die, which is exactly what happens, even though, despite his apparent myopia and the effects of the extreme cold on his body, he manages to construct the vital fire he needs. It's his lack of imagination that leads to his undoing, as his desperation, born of his present circumstances, prevents him from considering the consequences of building a fire beneath the boughs of snow that will ultimately fall onto the blaze and extinguish it. When this happens, it smothers his spirit as much as the fire and sends the man into a panic.

Growing up, every boy in my Cub Scout den knew how to build a fire using only a few basic materials. Later, while serving in the U.S. Marine Corps and out with my platoon on overnight field operations, my friends and I often built fires just so we could heat our otherwise bland MRE rations. Sometimes even today, I imagine myself lost in the jungles of South America, searching for a way out and having to build a fire at night just to keep the king of the jungle—the jaguar: pound for pound the most powerful of all the large cats—at bay. Would I do it? Could I do it? When in pain, or drenched from rain? Down on the leaves or up in the trees? I want to believe I could, but who's to say? After all, the jungle's so far away, although from my home on the southern Great Plains, maybe not as far as the northern woods of Maine.

Or Canada.

Imagine for a moment you're visiting the Great White North. Only it's summer and pleasant to be out in the forest, hiking or canoeing. Imagine too the initial anxiety and then dread washing over you when, coming upon a hill or bluff, you step up for a better view over the timber country surrounding you and spotting, a hundred miles away, a plume of smoke piping into the sky. Because the plume is so far away, it appears narrow and confined, perhaps even contained. But you know better. You know this plume is actually a wall of flames, twenty miles wide and growing with every new mile of forest it consumes. Which means you can't go around the fire, for soon it will surround you. You sense at once that you can't outrun it, that the fastest man or woman in the world couldn't possibly outrun it. But then you recall a certain lake, a clearing in the forest, half a day's paddle or hike away. You turn at once and make for this opening because it's your only chance in the world to survive the fire that the wind is pushing your way. By the time you arrive here, the fire is right on your heels, only a few miles behind you. Now imagine that you have the presence of mind to bury your belongings in the sand at the lake's edge, then to fill your canoe with rocks and submerge it. Now you get into the water beside the canoe and remain here until you begin to hear the fire's roar. You swim out into the lake, farther from the trees, farther from shore. Here, with your head just above the surface, you wait and watch the animals as they begin to emerge from the forest, first the rabbits—hundreds of them—followed by porcupines, deer, and bears, all scared, like you, and all running for their lives. All except for the rabbits and porcupines plunge into the water and remain there with their heads just above the surface as the fire reaches the lake with a roar, causing you to duck into the water to escape the heat again and again. Again and again you come up for air but the atmosphere is so hot you feel your lungs must be singed. The sky darkens. Embers flash through the air overhead, carried by the hot wind. Suddenly, the fire arcs over the water and the trees on the opposite side of the lake explode into flames. You see the terror in the eyes of the deer in the water beside you. Not far away are two moose, which you hadn't noticed before, and just beyond the moose, two bears. With fire as the greater danger, these animals have lost their natural fear of one another, and even of you.

An hour after the fire crosses the lake, as the forest continues to crackle and burn, you emerge from the water and attempt to dig up your belongings from the sand—your coat and your keys and wallet and knife and whatever else you might have brought with you into the North Woods. But the sand is still so hot you have to wait another hour before you can touch it. And because the surrounding woods are still smoldering, you'll be forced to camp on this night at the lake's edge, with the scent of smoke in your nose and the charred carcasses of all the rabbits that were afraid to enter the lake scattered along the shoreline. By now, the others, the large animals, have emerged from the water and wandered away down the beach, confused, stunned, bewildered by the fire.

This might be a hypothetical scenario and a fantastic one at that. But it's true and it may be one of the most gripping accounts of getting caught in a wildfire ever written. It happened many years ago to a prospector and lumber scout named John J. Rowlands, who wrote about it in his book *Cache Lake Country* (1947).

In Southern California, a debate rages over the issue of fire and its effects on the state's chaparral ecosystems—vast, often impenetrable shrublands found across the San Gabriel, San Bernardino, and Santa Cruz Mountains. According to the U.S. Forest Service, a combination of human development and fire suppression has led to a buildup of highly combustible fuels that pose a significant threat, especially in those low-buffer wildland-urban interfaces where homes have been constructed close to chaparral stands.

The California Chaparral Institute contends that because these ecosystems are shrubland rather than forest, they shouldn't be managed in the same way as forests or grasslands, which benefit from regular burning. Chaparral, the institute says, evolved through very intense, but infrequent, wildfires. Consequently, fires occurring in intervals of fifteen to twenty years or less can actually destroy the chaparral, one of California's most prominent ecosystems and a product of its Mediterranean-style climate.

According to the California Chaparral Institute, proper identification of chaparral as a shrub, and not a tree, is the first step toward a solution. Instead of the Los Padres National Forest, for example, the institute believes the area should be renamed the "Los Padres National Chaparral Recreation Area." Likewise for California's San Bernardino, Angeles, and Cleveland chaparral ecosystems, which are currently mislabeled as "forests."

Everyone seems to agree, however, that large, intense fires are natural, and therefore inevitable, for Southern California. And as is the case all across the West, these conflagrations will continue to have profound, and often devastating, consequences as modern society continues its encroachment into wild areas, with their abundance of naturally occurring combustible materials.

———

It took several days, but eventually my neighbors and I were able to breathe a collective sigh of relief as the big blaze to our east was contained and, finally, subdued by fire crews. Residents near Guthrie—Oklahoma's first capital and site of one of the state's first communities established in the wake of the 1889 Land Run—weren't so lucky. According to Reuters, the blaze torched roughly 3,500 acres, destroying thirty structures and forcing one thousand people to flee their homes. One person died in the fire.

———

Overdevelopment, including the expansion of housing, business complexes, and paved roadways, is a concern across the United States. It's particularly problematic in the Southeast, an area which, according to the *Washington Post*, has outpaced growth in the rest of the nation by 40 percent. Even more troubling is that this development has been primarily suburban, which not only consumes natural resources, displaces wildlife, and encourages runoff, but also contributes to global warming by increasing our dependence on automobiles.

Within this region, the Piedmont area between North Carolina and Georgia is particularly at risk. The U.S. Geological Survey reports that thousands of acres of forest and agricultural land between Raleigh and Atlanta could be lost to urban sprawl by the year 2060 if growth continues at its current pace. And why wouldn't it? According to the U.S. Census Bureau, the population of the United States, currently more than 318 million, has a net increase of one person every twelve seconds!

But whether it's done to house a swelling population or to expand our already bloated infrastructure of commercial centers or roadways, overdevelopment is always problematic, not only for what it creates, but also for the natural areas and wildlife habitat it destroys. And in doing so, it leaves those of us so inclined with fewer options to escape urban centers, which undermines our quality of life.

The Sierra Club defines "sprawl" as "low-density, automobile-dependent development beyond the edge of service and employment areas." This certainly describes the neighborhood, and entire city, where I live. It's such a problem that I'm trying to decide what to do about it. Should I buy a Prius? Should I move my family out of the suburbs and into the city? Even as I ponder this, the community continues to expand, such that my neighborhood, which twelve years ago was at the very edge of the city limits, is no longer so. Continuous development, building that slowed but never completely stopped during the 2008–2010 recession and that continues still, like a slow, smoldering blaze, has moved the fringe several miles to the north and insulated my subdivision in hundreds of acres of other, newer housing developments and paved roads.

Across the country it's more of the same. The Sierra Club reports that sprawl has become such a problem in Atlanta, for example, that it now leads the nation in the distance its motorists drive each day, while in Seattle, overdevelopment is undermining the water quality in Puget Sound, which is having an adverse effect on local fish and wildlife.

The Environmental Protection Agency says sprawl costs everyone, including residents of urban, suburban, and rural areas, through increased taxes, commuting time, automobile maintenance, and reduction in quality of life. It increases our dependence on automobiles to such an extent that an estimated 16 to 20 percent of household expenditures in the United States go to auto-related expenses.

The effect of sprawl on rural areas is even more troubling. Between 1970 and 1990, the United States lost nearly twenty million acres of countryside to development. The American Farmland Trust (AFT) tells us that less than one-fifth of U.S. land is considered "high-quality," and we're losing this precious resource at a rate of one acre every minute. Sprawl, the AFT says, devastates rural areas in particular by homogenizing formerly lush and diverse landscapes, by destroying our nation's agricultural heritage, and by undermining the economic and cultural identities of our small communities.

I'm reminded of that old Jethro Tull song "Farm on the Freeway," in which lead singer Ian Anderson laments the loss of his land, and thus his wealth. My hometown still struggles with the effects of sprawl. As new housing developments and shopping centers were constructed on the western edges of the city in the 1980s, downtown was nearly forgotten as business owners and shoppers abandoned the city center for the stores and restaurants closer to their new homes.

This problem isn't limited to the United States, and even developing countries like India and China seem unwilling to learn from our mistakes. *China Daily* reports that overdevelopment is destroying its country's cultural heritage through the demolition of historic architecture, which is being eliminated as China races to modernize its infrastructure.

Like the petroleum that powers most automobiles, the natural resources we expend to expand our human footprint are indeed finite and are in danger of disappearing. And like the looming "megalopolis" that threatens to displace the tranquil pine forests and bucolic fields between Atlanta and Raleigh, it's a problem that grows more and more acute the longer we ignore the ramifications of incessant and unsustainable development.

———

Several years ago, during the drought of 2011, a small, fast-moving wildfire swept through the neighborhood across the street from mine. The subdivision was still new then, with only a few homes, and the fire burned mostly empty lots and a wooden fence before being extinguished. Three weeks later green grass shoots could be seen protruding from the charred ground, and soon small shrubs began to appear. Not long thereafter, these lots were leveled in preparation for the paved streets and new homes that would come. Today, as I jog through the neighborhood, the only indications of a fire are these sprawling brick homes, which smell not like smoke, but sawdust and cement.

AMONG URBAN TREES

Of the two largest land tracts that make up the bulk of the city park system in Edmond, Oklahoma, I have a strong preference for E. C. Hafer Park, situated just south of busy Second Street on the east side of Bryant Avenue, because it's so heavily wooded. When my son, Jackson, was in elementary school, he liked to stop at Hafer so he could play on the swings. Though today he's a busy teenager, Jackson still enjoys the swings, although we don't visit the park as often as we used to. When we do, it's generally to stretch our legs on the paved trail that circles the facility's perimeter. Sometimes in early spring I bring my camera and tripod, and as Jackson swings and my wife, Ellen, walks the trail, I enjoy photographing the blooming tulips and other flowers the city plants along the walkway. And while there is much to enjoy about the small duck pond, where children are permitted to cast to catfish and bass, which, strangely, I've never seen anyone catch, I consider the park's abundant trees its greatest feature.

Whereas Mitch Park, on the city's northern fringes, mirrors the expansive, gently rolling, and sparsely treed western Oklahoma plains, Hafer Park has been carved, essentially, from the Cross Timbers, the ancient forest of stout, low-growing post oaks and blackjacks that extends from eastern Kansas across central and southern Oklahoma and well into Texas. Though large swaths of these ironclad trees were cleared for farming in the nineteenth century, much of the Cross Timbers remains intact, comprising one of our country's most unadulterated forests.

It's easy to overlook these short, rugged trees. In central Oklahoma, where I live, they're everywhere. Interstate 35, which bisects the state, essentially dividing it in half, seems to be the demarcation line. To the west, the plains open up and unfold virtually treeless into Texas and New Mexico. East of I-35, in central and southern Oklahoma, however, the Cross Timbers forest blankets the landscape in a mosaic of post oak and blackjack so thick one would have a tough time moving through it without the aid of, say, a herd of brush-clearing goats. Given the ubiquity of these trees and the lack of publicity they're afforded, even many Oklahomans fail to recognize their significance. After all, Oklahoma is on the southern Great Plains. Forests, especially ancient ones, are products of places like northern California and Alaska, aren't they?

According to the Arkansas Tree-Ring Laboratory, "many . . . do not realize that ancient forests survive extensively across the rugged terrain of the southern plains, but the Cross Timbers do not satisfy the stereotype for ancient forests, which remains fixated on giant redwoods or massive hardwoods."

This landscape of slow-growing trees, which evolved in the presence of (and in spite of) regular droughts, contains millions of post oaks two hundred to four hundred years old—living specimens that predate the birth of our nation—as well as, along some fire-protected bluff lines, redcedar trees over five hundred years old.

The Cross Timbers forest skirts the eastern fringe of Edmond, Oklahoma, constituting one of the region's predominant physical features. Despite Hafer Park's scattered open pockets, which have been cleared to facilitate the building of a trail system, and the open glades for children's playground equipment, picnic tables, and so forth, much of the 121-acre park has been left in a dense forest of post oaks and blackjack oaks. This urban forest is crisscrossed with meandering miles of dirt trails, which hikers and perhaps a few adventurous mountain bikers enjoy using. Beyond these narrow, twisting paths, however, the Hafer Park forest is unimproved. There are no trail markers, no signs, no orienteering aids. This was part of the attraction for Jackson and me one autumn Saturday, as we decided to explore this insulated forest-within-the-larger-Cross-Timbers-forest. The other attraction, I suppose, was curiosity: Why, in designing the park, had the city chosen to leave such a large swath of it undeveloped? What would we find inside this tantalizing stand of woods? What types of wildlife made their home here? And, maybe most importantly, was this urban forest a valued feature of the park, like the playgrounds and duck pond, or was it simply undeveloped space awaiting its own date with the blueprints and bulldozers?

As we left the paved trail and followed a narrow, twisting, hard-packed dirt path into the trees, I felt a sense of wonder, for this intriguing forest, which was surrounded on every side at some distance or another by expansive homes, stores, restaurants, and other signs of civilization, was a survivor of the development that has so altered, and in many cases degraded, our nation's landscape over the past two centuries. Though it seems this land had once been used for agricultural purposes and many of the original trees cleared, the forest had been given a second chance.

Also there was a sense of nostalgia, as the Hafer Park forest reminded me very much of the immense tracts of undeveloped and unspoiled woodlands surrounding the remote country home I lived in for a short period during my teenage years.

As we rounded a bend in the trail, leaving the pavement and civilization temporarily behind, I felt very much like a kid again.

———

When Ellen and I were shopping for our first house together, we were attracted to an older, established neighborhood in central

Norman, Oklahoma. Not only were the modest-sized, midcentury ranch-style homes appealing, but the area was blanketed with mature trees. The house we eventually purchased had a towering oak in the front yard, and the quarter-dollar-sized acorns it produced must have delighted the squirrels. There were various trees scattered across our backyard, and these, combined with others on neighboring properties, served to shade our home in the afternoons. It was a good thing, because our little air-conditioning unit struggled to keep the house cool on summer days. At the time, we couldn't afford to replace it, and we relied heavily on the home warranty the sellers had provided when we purchased the property. Two or three times every summer we would have to call the air-conditioner repairman—who was an employee of the company that had provided the warranty. After four or five visits, I began to wonder whether he might reasonably conclude that our forty-year-old AC unit needed to be replaced, and that doing so would be in everyone's best interest.

That didn't happen.

Instead, we continued to call the repairman every time the unit stalled, seemed on the verge of blowing up, or otherwise proved itself unfit for the task of cooling our little house. And the repairman continued to come out and service the condenser again and again, rather than replace it. Although summer is my favorite season, there were times I found myself dreading the afternoons, when temperatures would soar to a hundred degrees or more. What carried us through those long, hot Oklahoma summers, more than anything, were the trees that shaded our home for much of the day and kept the house five, ten, maybe fifteen degrees cooler than it would have been without them.

According to American Forests, a national nonprofit conservation organization advocating for the protection and expansion of our nation's forests, having just three mature trees around your home, two on the west side and another on the east, can provide enough shade to reduce your cooling costs by 30 percent. And when they're situated so as to reduce your home's exposure to the wind, trees can help mitigate heating costs by nearly 10 percent.

But reducing our energy demands is only one benefit of urban trees. A 2012 report by the U.S. Forest Service noted that "two medium-sized, healthy trees can supply the oxygen required by a single person over the course of a year." Additionally, urban trees in the lower United States have been found to remove nearly eight hundred thousand tons of air pollution annually from the atmosphere.

Trees also aid in water management. American Forests reports that a single tree can intercept 760 gallons of rainwater, helping reduce runoff and flooding. Given that our cities have so many impermeable spaces such as paved parking lots and streets, rain accumulates quickly rather than being absorbed into the ground, which means that even ordinary rainfall events can lead to flash floods. Trees capture much of this rain, however, allowing it to be absorbed into the roots and soil. In this sense, trees reduce a city's need to construct artificial stormwater controls, which saves the community money.

Additionally, trees help filter this water. As rainwater flows across pavement, it picks up pollutants, which can end up in our streams and waterways. Trees help purify this runoff by absorbing the collected contaminants.

Perhaps just as importantly, trees filter noise and increase quality of life in our cities, for both humans and wildlife. A 2003 report from the *Journal of Arboriculture* noted that "a stronger sense of community and empowerment to improve neighborhood conditions in inner cities has been attributed to involvement in urban forestry efforts." Evidently, despite the habitats of concrete and glass that we construct for ourselves, humankind's evolution

among trees and green spaces continues to have a positive and profound effect on even society's most urban denizens. As humans,
we're intrinsically linked to the natural world, however much we
may shield ourselves from it.

This may be more evident now than ever. As our planet warms,
trees are becoming increasingly important for their ability to mitigate climate change. They do this through carbon sequestration
and by helping reduce the amounts of greenhouse gases emitted.
Trees and shrubs absorb carbon, storing it in woody tissues for
decades or even centuries. And this is significant. According to
a 2002 article in *Environmental Pollution*, "Carbon Storage and
Sequestration by Urban Trees in the USA," urban trees in the
lower forty-eight states store some 770 million tons of carbon,
which reflected a value of over $14 billion at the time the article
was published, and likely more today.

It's important to note that "urban forests" include not only isolated woodlots and large stands of trees such as those in Hafer Park,
but also street trees, gardens, landscaped avenues, greenbelts, river
and creek corridors, nature preserves, wetlands, and trees planted
at former industrial sites. The U.S. Forest Service notes that urban
trees provide "a return three times greater than tree-care costs" and
are the basis for the green infrastructure on which communities
depend. Which makes all our urban trees important. Every single
one.

———

Civilization disappeared surprisingly quickly as Jackson and I
entered the Hafer Park forest. After only a few paces down the narrow dirt path, we were ensconced in the incredibly dense Oklahoma
Cross Timbers. It was a beautiful, sunny day in early October. The
park was crowded—at least the western half of it, which contains
the playground equipment, artificial rock-climbing wall, and duck
pond. Although I couldn't see them, I could hear children playing

and people laughing in the distance. There was the hissing din of faraway traffic, which grew more and more faint the deeper into the forest we walked. The trees were still foliated at this time of year, though the leaves were beginning to lose their verdant sheen.

We noticed a few footprints on some of the trails, and at one point we spotted the knobby-tire tracks of a mountain bike. The paths threaded through the trees, frequently intersecting others, and twisting and turning and veering off in new directions. We saw dog tracks—or were they coyote prints?—and later the smaller, rounded, contracted-claw tracks of a bobcat. At one point Jackson commented that this was fun. "I feel like we're hiding in here," he said. "We are," I said. "That's why the animals like it in here. This is where they feel safe."

————

For the past twelve years my family has lived in a house whose backyard borders a small creek. Across the creek is a field, which is insulated on two sides by isolated woodlots. In late autumn we often see deer moving back and forth between these stands of trees. Sometimes the deer dart across the open field; other times they use the funnel of riparian trees growing along the edge of the creek as cover. It's fun to watch them, and it pleases me to know that even here in this suburban Oklahoma City bedroom community, we've left—or overlooked, or otherwise failed to develop—enough microhabitat to support even large animals like white-tailed deer.

In my own backyard we've seen everything from coyotes, foxes, bobcats, and the occasional stray dog to beavers, skunks, opossums, raccoons, and of course innumerable squirrels and bird species. Aside from wildlife habitat, the funnel of trees growing along the creek serves another important purpose: erosion control. The creek fills quickly during a prolonged or intense rainfall, and at such times I'm always grateful for these trees and the stream-side vegetation, knowing their roots are helping retain the soil that the swift currents would otherwise carve away from the banks and wash downstream. Once, during an event the area's leading meteorologist called a "five-hundred-year flood," the creek rose so high it threatened to spill over the banks. Had it not been for these stalwart oaks and elms and redbuds, the creek would have been in my backyard.

Though it's no more than thirty feet across in some places, this strip of trees is thick enough during the warm months that you can't see the creek on the other side. And the vegetation does a wonderful job of absorbing traffic noise from nearby roadways.

Each year the trees shading my backyard grow just a bit taller and broader, which means they block progressively more sunlight from reaching my lawn. As a result, the Bermuda grass, which thrives in open spaces where it can receive abundant sunshine, has thinned, forcing me to plant more and more shade-tolerant fescue. I like the Bermuda better, although the fescue greens up earlier in the year and retains its color well into autumn. But what choice do I have, considering that more and more of my backyard is shaded during peak sunlight hours?

Despite this, and the blanket of leaves that find their way into my yard every autumn, I wouldn't want to lose the trees, for they attract so many beautiful birds to my backyard.

This spring, we've had wave after wave of cedar waxwings, those elegant birds with the thin black masks, almost neon-bright yellow tips on their tail feathers, and wing tips splashed in red, as they migrate north. They appear in groups of ten to twenty birds at a time, gracing my trees with their presence.

Cardinals, blue jays, robins: these are year-round residents in central Oklahoma, and I delight in watching them color my backyard as they flutter through the trees and across my lawn. Ditto the red-bellied and downy woodpeckers. When I have the feeders set out during winter, the tufted titmouse, one of my favorite birds, alights on the perch, takes a seed in its neat black beak, and flies away to a nearby limb where it cracks the shell and eats the contents before returning to the feeder to repeat the process. Same with our chickadee-dee-dees. Some birds, like mourning doves, show up in pairs and together they scour the lawn for food. I love watching the two Bewick's wrens—we have both Bewick's and Carolinas where I live—that appear daily on my back porch. They hop around the furniture, the grill, the windowsills as they hunt for insects. I've seen them scale the brick wall to snatch a spider or some tiny morsel. I'm always grateful for their extermination services, and with their frenetic movements and inquisitive expressions and those long, jaunting tail feathers, they seem almost like cartoon characters. I so enjoy seeing them.

Without the trees in my backyard we wouldn't have many birds, and for this, and the fact that my office doubles as an excellent bird blind, allowing me unobstructed views of this vital microhabitat, I'm reluctant to live anywhere else.

———

At some point I realized we were lost. Initially, I found this hard to believe. As someone who has spent a great deal of his life outdoors, in and among trees and forests and woodlands, it was a bit embarrassing. Not only this, but given that Hafer Park is only 121 acres in size, and considering that approximately one-third of the park (my estimate) has been left in unimproved forest and woodlands, that meant we were lost in a small, isolated pocket of urban trees, surrounded on every side by civilization. How could this be? I wondered.

The tight, twisting, hard-packed trails are how it came to be. Not only the trails but also, and perhaps more importantly, the acres of thick, dense post oaks and blackjack oaks surrounding them, trees so thick that once we rounded the first bend, effectively insulating ourselves from the larger park, we were enveloped in the Oklahoma Cross Timbers, a miniature forest, temporarily cut off from civilization and left to fend for ourselves until we could find a way out. It gave me a bit of anxiety at first. Then I took a deep breath, looked around, and mentioned to Jackson that we were lost. "How we gonna get out, then?" he asked. "We'll find a way," I said.

At this point being lost began to seem like a minor challenge, which I found strangely appealing. I wouldn't have chosen to get lost in an urban park in, *ahem*, my city of current residence. But I told myself that maybe this was less an obstacle than an opportunity. An opportunity to show Jackson how to conduct oneself in the event one becomes lost, or rather, *disoriented*, in an urban park in his current city of residence.

"Listen," I said. "Try to find the direction those voices are coming from."

We could still hear people talking and laughing, but they were more distant than before and their voices seemed to emanate from several directions. There was quite a bit of ground and trees separating us, and there was no clear path to the other side of the park. It was as if we were trying to find our way out of one of those theme-park mazes with all the mirrors. And considering the meandering nature of the trails, and the fact that they frequently bisected other paths, looping in and out, back and forth, we had no idea which one to follow.

So I used the sun's position in the sky to try to gauge the direction I thought was east, the direction leading to the walkway we'd come in on, and which I thought would be the closest, fastest path out of the trees. We headed that way. The forest was so dense we couldn't see more than a few feet into it in any direction. However, this being the Cross Timbers, and these post oaks and blackjacks being only twenty-five or so feet in height, we were able to see above them for some distance. As we skirted the trails, I kept my eye on the skyline above, knowing we'd eventually find something to use as a reference point or landmark to which we could navigate.

The fact that we couldn't easily find one suggested to me that this urban forest was a feature of Hafer Park, a valuable component of this public space and no different in this respect from the children's playground or the artificial rock-climbing wall. The fact that it likely finds more use by wild animals and birds than by humans spoke to its ability to meet diverse needs. And best of all, no taxpayer dollars had been spent to develop it. Still, in this day and age when undeveloped land is usually valued more for its economic potential than anything else, I wondered whether the city of Edmond had plans to alter this natural feature of the park.

Recently, I put the question to Craig Dishman, the city's director of parks and recreation, who told me that Edmond has no plans to develop the area with any amenities. Not that any are needed, as far as I can see. "The only thing I could envision is a few more unpaved trails cutting through to the other side," Dishman said, "but not on our list anytime soon."

This was good to hear because these woods help make Hafer Park special, and as the city continues to expand on every side, this isolated stand of Cross Timbers becomes increasingly significant. It's like a living history museum that's open to the public every day of the week, and exploring it regularly, even if only from the paved walking trail, is better than any medicine I know of.

Every few minutes we would stop and listen, hoping that we'd hear the sounds of the park becoming progressively clearer. They remained distant and vague, however. I was grateful it was a calm day, sunny with only a light breeze. Had it gusted to twenty miles per hour or more, as it so often does in Oklahoma, we would have heard only the howling wind and rattling tree branches. As it was, the distant voices were reassuring, reminding us that we weren't too far lost, that we weren't alone.

The thought occurred to me that we could be walking in circles, although I focused on keeping the sun just off my right shoulder, which meant we had to be heading east. And as we moved along the trail, I pointed to the treetops, telling Jackson to keep looking for a landmark, something we could use as an orienteering aid.

Neither of us had a cell phone with us that day. I almost never carry mine, and Jackson had left his in the car. Why would we need a cell phone? Certainly not to call for help; we were at the park, after all, an *urban* park. Rather, I figured Jackson's fancy smartphone might have a compass, although I still felt reasonably certain about the direction we were traveling, and I was sure that if we kept it up we'd come out on the east side of the park. And yet the longer we went without spotting a landmark, without hearing nearby voices, doubt began to infiltrate my mind. I didn't mention this to Jackson. I simply told him to keep scanning the treetops around us, to keep listening, even as we continued moving through the trees. Had we been lost in a much larger and more remote forest, one of us would have climbed a tree to try to spot a landmark. And if none were found, I suppose we would have remained in one place, as one is supposed to do to make it easier for searchers to find you. But we were in an urban forest in a city park. We weren't lost, I told myself, so much as momentarily disoriented, so much as tempo-rarily challenged.

Some time later we spotted the power-line towers that I knew skirted the eastern edge of the park. I pointed them out to Jackson and we headed in that direction. Moments later we emerged from the trees and onto the paved walking trail, into what seemed a very different and much more familiar world. It was virtually silent on this side of the park. The sun was waning in the west; the park was winding down for the day. Jackson and I headed back to the car, following the walking trail through the trees. We didn't encounter anyone else along the way until we arrived in the parking lot. Had we been a couple of hours later in spotting the electric tower, it's possible we may have had to spend the night in Hafer Park, as incredible as it sounds. The more I thought about this possibility, however, the more I appreciated this piece of the Cross Timbers. For an urban forest's greatest benefit may be the opportunity it affords us to unplug from civilization and lose ourselves, even unintentionally, even temporarily, in the natural world that lingers to some extent in all of us.

OH, GIVE ME A HOME . . .

The other day I was working at the kitchen table. It was a sunny afternoon, the autumn air cool and crisp. As I often do when the weather is so agreeable, I raised a couple of the kitchen windows and delighted in the fresh air and the sounds of the breeze whistling through the trees in my backyard.

After a while the wind gusted and there came a creaking noise, which increased in pitch within the span of a few seconds, growing louder and more pronounced, suggesting movement and force. Then the noise abated, leaving in its place a hushed moment of anticipation, the kind that heralds a sudden and powerful crash. I looked up from my work toward the narrow strip of riparian woods lining one side of my backyard like a tall, dense fence, searching for the source of the creaking noise, looking for the movement or displacement that corresponded to the unmistakable high-pitched sound I'd just heard. And I spotted it, there through the woods, beside the creek, as a large tree leaned and fell to the ground. This was certainly a surprise. It seemed the wind was stronger than I'd realized. So I got up and went outside to investigate. Picking my way through the trees, I came out on the creek bank and noticed, along with the newly felled tree, scattered wood chips seasoning the blanket of leaves and grasses, and a freshly gnawed tree stump. Beavers. I'd never noticed them. Where had they come from? How many were here? I was surprised to realize beavers were living in this suburban creek, surrounded by human civilization on every side. Maybe they'd been here all along, quietly going about their business, although this seemed unlikely. I'd never noticed any dams or conically chewed stumps. I imagined they were recent arrivals, having just migrated into the neighborhood. Or maybe I should say they'd *returned* to this area, for they've been here on the southern Great Plains much longer than we have.

In *A Tour on the Prairies*, Washington Irving wrote of seeing a beaver dam while on his 1832 expedition through present-day Oklahoma. "In the course of the morning we crossed a deep stream with a complete beaver dam, above three feet high, making a large pond, and doubtless containing several families of that industrious animal, although not one showed his nose above water," he writes. "The Captain would not permit this amphibious commonwealth to be disturbed."

I am intrigued by this admission and the captain's obvious respect for the welfare of these beavers. Today, despite being Canada's national emblem, where their image appears, among other places, on the country's five-cent coin, and despite being the official mascot for Oregon State University, the City College of New York, the London School of Economics, and probably many other schools and organizations, beavers don't get much respect, especially when they build their homes close to our own. The coauthors of *Mammals of Oklahoma* (1989), William Caire, Jack Tyler, Bryan Glass, and Michael Mares, explain that beavers were once widespread across North America, but that trapping, especially during the late nineteenth century, reduced them nearly to extinction.

In his *Journal of Travels*, English botanist Thomas Nuttall noted the ease with which these industrious rodents were trapped. "Scarcely any thing [sic] is now employed for bait but the musk or castoreum of the animal itself," he writes. "As they live in community, they are jealous and hostile to strangers of their own species, and following the scent of the bait, are deceived into the trap."

Detailing his adventures exploring present-day Arkansas and eastern Oklahoma, Nuttall writes of suffering from a fever one afternoon, which forced him to seek shade and rest, while his traveling partner took the opportunity to trap for beaver, catching four of these animals in one night. Additionally, in his entry for March 12, 1819, he writes of encountering "captain Prior [sic] and Mr. Richards, descending (the Arkansas River) with cargoes of furs and peltries, collected among the Osages."

Beavers had been relentlessly hunted and trapped for centuries, not only in the New World but also in Europe and Asia. When populations of the once-prolific European beaver dwindled in the seventeenth century, North American beaver pelts began to supply the European market, where they were in great demand, especially in England and France, for the making of hats. Beaver fur was particularly desirable for the hatting industry because it was so well suited to the production of felt, the basic material used in hats. J. F. Crean, writing in the *Canadian Journal of Economics and Political Science*, calls beaver fur the "raw material *par excellence* for felt," noting that beaver felt is both tight and supple, and more durable under heavy wear, even when wet, than that made from other furs. "Hence, before the technological revolution introduced by carroting," Crean writes, "beaver fur was the only material which would permit the manufacture of a hat with a large and durable brim."

Beaver fur did more than clothe us, however. It also sustained the economies of early North American colonies and was the basis for trade between many Native American tribes and European explorers and settlers. According to an Oklahoma Historical Society article by Brad Agnew, "Fur Trappers and Traders," the fur trade was instrumental in the development of the region that would eventually become Oklahoma, and the trading posts located at the confluence of the Arkansas, Grand, and Verdigris Rivers, an area known as the "Three Forks," became a hub for commercial activity between Native Americans and European explorers, traders, and frontiersmen. "At trading posts near the Three Forks trade goods from the Illinois country and New Orleans were exchanged for pelts of beaver, deer, bison, and other furbearing animals," Agnew writes.

The nineteenth century saw the decline of the fur trade, however, and in the late 1800s, as the American bison was being slaughtered and eliminated from its native home on the Great Plains, the beaver was reaching a critical juncture in its own history. As with the European beaver, centuries of unregulated trapping and hunting had finally brought the North American beaver to the brink of extinction.

In the twentieth century, remnant populations of beavers gradually expanded, and along with restocking efforts and the establishment of game laws that effectively ended unregulated trapping, the animals made a comeback. Today beavers are found throughout Oklahoma and much of the United States. It's a success story, I suppose, so long as they aren't felling your trees to construct their lodges and dams.

Not long after I realized beavers had returned to my creek, a neighbor told me he'd lost trees to these diligent rodents. Riparian trees that skirt creeks and streams, especially those flowing through neighborhoods, suburban communities, and cities the world over, perform many valuable functions. They provide shade. They buffer sound from nearby roadways. They provide a natural and attractive screen between homes and other neighborhoods. And, maybe most importantly, they help prevent erosion. When heavy rains transform streams from lazy trickles into wild torrents, riparian vegetation, especially trees, helps maintain the integrity of the stream banks, preventing them from crumbling and washing away.

Also, these vegetation corridors provide vital wildlife habitat for coyotes, bobcats, red and gray foxes, raccoons, opossums, skunks, armadillos, squirrels, white-tailed deer, and many other species. All these animals use the riparian woods for cover. Some make their homes in these narrow funnels of urban forest. Some hunt here. Others, like the deer, use the trees to conceal their movements when traveling. But in every case, riparian vegetation is vital for wildlife, especially in urban and suburban areas, where natural habitat is fragmented, at best.

The number of resident and migrating birds using riparian trees for food and shelter is even more extensive, and these may include robins, cardinals, blue jays, titmice, sparrows, vireos, juncos, doves, bluebirds, wrens, waxwings, buntings, woodpeckers, thrashers, hawks, kites, kestrels, owls, and hundreds of others.

Like many homeowners, I treasure the riparian trees in my neighborhood, both for the natural buffer they offer from other homes and nearby roadways, and for the habitat they provide for wildlife. So do my neighbors. Which is why it was inevitable, I suppose, that my neighborhood hired a professional trapper to remove the beavers from my creek.

The neighborhood board of directors sent an email to residents, explaining the situation and asking parents to keep their children out of the creek for the next several weeks, until the beavers could be removed. "Traps can be dangerous to children or pets," the email warned. "Please avoid the creek until the beavers have been successfully removed."

Beavers aren't the only animals that have been hunted or trapped to the point of extinction here in Oklahoma. American bison once roamed our vast, rolling fields in enormous herds, sharing these frontier lands with elk, bears, wolves, mountain lions, wild horses, and even a few alligators. As with the beaver, populations of these species dwindled with European settlement of the southern plains in the nineteenth century. Though today black bears are returning to eastern Oklahoma, and though a few hundred alligators, including some surprisingly large ones, still call the Sooner State home, viable, wild populations of most of these once-prolific animals remain absent from the state.

Regrettably, we're doing the same thing to butterflies and bees with our use of pesticides and herbicides. And when our pollinators are gone, we're in real trouble.

Despite society's ongoing assault on the natural world, however, I'm inclined to believe we can mitigate, and in some cases even reverse, the ecological damage human activity has caused over the past century or more.

A case in point: the July 1–4, 2016, "Holiday edition" of *USA Today* reported that the worldwide ban on chlorofluorocarbons (CFCs), chemicals once commonly used as refrigerants for air conditioners and as aerosol propellants in cans of hair spray and deodorant, was helping repair the much-publicized "hole" in the earth's protective ozone layer. Though ozone is a damaging pollutant when found in the lower atmosphere, near the ground, in the stratosphere it shields the earth from harmful ultraviolet solar radiation. In the 1980s, scientists showed that CFC-released chlorine in the stratosphere was destroying the earth's ozone layer. This led to the 1989 signing of the Montreal Protocol, the international treaty that phased out CFCs, which time has proven effective. As the *USA Today* article explained, researchers found that the hole in the earth's ozone layer had shrunk by more than 1.5 million square miles—roughly half the area of the contiguous United States—since 2000, when ozone depletion was most acute. "The discovery shows global attempts to improve Earth's environment can work," writes the author, Doyle Rice, "providing a template for how humanity could tackle the exponentially larger issue of climate change."

Or our oceans' rapidly declining fish stocks.

In his book *Four Fish*, author Paul Greenberg calls the once-ubiquitous cod a "workaday fish, the fish upon which average people rely for their daily meal," whose "white flaky flesh nourished humanity from medieval times through the discovery of the Americas and on into the industrial era," and perhaps most revealingly, one whose "very abundance is its most notable characteristic."

Because of commercial overfishing, however, by 1994 most cod stocks were considered "collapsed," a term indicating the loss of 90 percent of the fish's historical population. That same year, the U.S. government closed the greatest New England fishing grounds, Georges Bank, to commercial cod fishing. Just as the thoughtless, wholesale killing of the once-prolific passenger pigeon led to its extirpation early in the twentieth century, so too had ignorance and greed ravaged a species that, like the passenger pigeon, was once so abundant that many considered it inexhaustible. The main difference was that unlike the case with the passenger pigeon, which was wiped off the face of the planet never to return again, there were still a few cod around.

The New England cod crisis led to the formation of the Sustainable Fisheries Act, which, as Greenberg writes, "essentially *required* that overfishing be ended for every single American fish or shellfish." It also established goals and timelines for the rebuilding of commercial fish stocks. The result of all this, according to Greenberg, is that Gulf of Maine and Georges Bank haddock populations are now considered fully rebuilt, while Gulf of Maine codfish are halfway to their rebuilding goal. The Georges Bank cod population was so decimated that its rebuilding timeline has been extended to 2026, which means it may be too early to tell how this stock is faring.

Clearly, there is reason to be optimistic about the future of our oceans. While we hear much about declining fish stocks, Greenberg writes that "the examples of science-based successes are marked, accurately documented, and replicable." And just as important, the world's oceans, unlike many of our landscapes, remain reclaimable. According to *National Geographic*, sprawl consumes more than two million acres of rural land in the United States each year. But as the commercial fishing ban in New England waters suggests, marine ecosystems, when liberated from human exploitation, tend to recover over time.

So, too, do birds. After DDT was outlawed in the early 1970s, the bald eagle made a strong comeback and appears to be thriving today, having been removed from the federal lists of threatened and endangered species. But what of the millions of birds displaced as a result of agricultural land conversion and urbanization? Although bird populations often experience dramatic declines at the onset of new suburban development, evidence suggests that as a neighborhood's newly planted trees gradually grow and mature, they become progressively more attractive to birds. Biologist Frederick R. Gehlbach documented as much in his book *Mountain Islands and Desert Seas: A Natural History of the U.S.-Mexican Borderlands* (1981), citing twenty-five-year-old suburban developments in Claremont, California, where avifaunal diversity was nearly 80 percent of that in nearby chaparral communities, and seventy-year-old areas of the same city featuring bird populations reflecting 86 percent of the region's natural diversity. "Perhaps an urban bird community diversifies and becomes more interesting as a city ages," he writes.

What this suggests is that there is indeed hope for our wild neighbors, provided that we can find it within ourselves to modify our own activities and behavior. Sustainability, after all, is not just a trendy buzzword, but more importantly a concept marked by the capacity to endure over time. Given that we rely on nature in many ways to help meet both our economic and cultural needs, and considering that our natural surroundings provide a quality-of-life-enhancing aesthetic value for all of us, the concept of sustainability is vital to our society's ability to prosper and progress going forward. This is reflected in the "land ethic" for which Aldo Leopold so famously advocated in *A Sand County Almanac*, whereby humankind's role changes from that of conqueror of the land community (which includes, according to Leopold, "soils, waters, plants, and animals") to a member and citizen of it. "It implies respect for his fellow members," he writes, "and also respect for the community as such."

The truth is, a civilized society is one that respects not only human life and dignity, but also natural environments and the myriad life forms that sustain and nourish us.

———

It took about a month. Gradually, I stopped seeing the trapper's pickup truck and I knew the neighborhood had won the battle. For now. But the beavers will be back. Of this I have no doubt.

Sometimes I think we react too quickly when we discover wildlife living in such proximity to our own homes. Very often, we tend to try to manage nature, to remove these animals and relocate them. But one of the best quality-of-life indicators I know of is a landscape teeming with native flora and fauna, which is the mark of both a healthy ecosystem and a society that recognizes the immeasurable value such areas provide for humans and wildlife.

Mohandas Gandhi is often credited with having said, "The greatness of a nation and its moral progress can be judged by the way its animals are treated." Surely, he meant all animals.

BIRDS OF SUMMER

I. MIGRATION

The kite likes warm weather . . .
by mid-September most of the kites have gone.

—GEORGE MIKSCH SUTTON, *Fifty Common Birds
of Oklahoma and the Southern Great Plains*

The wind was ripping in from the ocean, rippling the aviators' flight suits and funneling beneath their hang gliders' bright wings—if one can call eighteen or twenty feet of brightly colored, aluminum-framed, trampoline-taut nylon, "wings"—giving lift and sudden life to these exotically minimalist aircraft. I was standing on the cliffs overlooking the Pacific Ocean as a small procession of gliders waited their turn on the runway—a grassy meadow sloping gently toward the sea. A boy from the plains, I wasn't used to such heights, and every time I glanced down at the beach and the sunbathers and surfers hundreds of feet below, I felt a bit dizzy. I wondered how these daredevils could leap off the cliff, how they could trust their lives to such simple equipment. Mostly, I wondered what it would be like to fly, to glide through the sky without an engine, with the sea breeze swirling around you, the salty marine air filling your nose, viewing the coast on the wing, like a bird.

Finally, I took a step back, and as I did the first pilot sprinted toward the sea and sky, leaping off the cliff into the Southern

California sunshine. There was an excited cheer from the small crowd, and a then few sharp whistles as the wind seized the glider and lifted it. Magically, the pilot was circling overhead, now veering out over the ocean, now turning and soaring over the grassy meadow from which he'd just taken off, spiraling in the bright sky, his nylon flight suit rippling silently as he glided higher and higher, like a young bird that has just found its wings, awkward but efficient, and becoming more confident, more capable, more free and independent with each minute in the air.

It was the summer of 1989 and I'd just arrived at Camp Pendleton in Southern California for my occupational training. I was nineteen, a new Marine, fresh from boot camp and not long out of the nest back in Oklahoma. Part of the appeal of watching these aircraft, besides the fact that it cost nothing to do so, was their silence and simplicity. They bore no motors. No noisy, smelly, fuel-consuming, toxin-producing engines. Their primary feature was their broad nylon wings. The only fuel needed was wind, which propelled these prehistoric-looking contraptions and their human cargo into seemingly effortless flight. Standing on the cliffs and watching them take off and glide through the coastal skies was to feel the spirit soar, was to fly vicariously. I took many such flights that summer.

By September I had completed my training and left Southern California for the East Coast. As far as I could tell, there was no hang gliding here. Nor was I aware of any back home on the southern plains, although we certainly had the wind for it. I suppose I never thought about those gliders again until I spotted Mississippi kites circling high above me as I swam on my back one hot summer day many years later. Though there were other birds about, and some of them, like the mockingbird, were quite vocal, the kites had my attention because I recognized them from previous summers, and also because they flew with such ease and grace. Other than an occasional high-pitched *Phee, phew!* these birds were silent as they glided and wheeled through the sky, so high and free and elegant. They looked as if they could remain aloft indefinitely. It was a treat to watch them.

I was delighted to learn that Mississippi kites (*Ictinia mississippiensis*) migrate from South America to the southern United States each summer for nesting. In recent years it seems they've expanded their range in the United States and are now being spotted as far north as New England on the East Coast. Yet the southern plains region appears to be particularly attractive to these raptors. George Miksch Sutton included the Mississippi kite in his book *Fifty Common Birds of Oklahoma and the Southern Great Plains* (1977), writing that these birds were "downright common in parts of western Oklahoma." By the early 1990s, the kites had become "locally common in central and western Oklahoma," according to Frederick M. and A. Marguerite Baumgartner, who noted in their book *Oklahoma Bird Life* (1992) that the Sooner State is home to the highest population densities of Mississippi kites on the North American continent.

This was certainly cause for celebration, as it meant I was in the ideal location in which to observe the birds, a fact reinforced by the numerous kites patrolling the skies above me that day at the swimming pool.

Not long after the kites arrived in central Oklahoma in the spring of 2016, I began mentally mapping the locations of their nesting trees in my neighborhood and observing them every chance I got. They were everywhere, soaring high above me as I jogged, perched on treetop branches as I walked the dogs. Every time I'd go outside, from midmorning until early evening, I was certain of seeing kites floating through the sky.

But alas, in late May I had to leave for the East Coast to research another project I was working on. I ended up spending the first half of the summer there. When I returned to Oklahoma in late July, the adult kites filled the sky as before, but now they were consumed with feeding their young. They would soar through the air, catch a cicada or dragonfly, and return to their nests to feed their fast-growing fledglings. A few weeks later, toward the end of summer, they began departing our area, eight, ten, twelve birds at a time. Our skies emptied more and more every day until, at some point in late September, the kites had all gone away just as surely as our summer.

II. DESCRIPTION AND ETYMOLOGY

> One of the smaller hawks, the Mississippi Kite
> is a creature of infinite grace and beauty.
>
> —FREDERICK M. AND A. MARGUERITE BAUMGARTNER,
> *Oklahoma Bird Life*

Of all the descriptions of the Mississippi kite I've read or heard, this one, from Frederick M. and A. Marguerite Baumgartner's *Oklahoma Bird Life*, is my favorite. The Mississippi kite: a creature of infinite grace and beauty. I love that, and it's so accurate.

As raptors go, it is indeed small. It's about the size of a pigeon, according to Rondi Large, executive director of WildCare Oklahoma, a nonprofit organization that rehabilitates dozens (and sometimes hundreds) of Mississippi kites each year, as well as many other types of wildlife. On a recent visit to WildCare, Rondi showed my son, Jackson, and me some of the injured kites in her care. Most were young birds, in their buff and barred juvenile plumage, and surprisingly tolerant of us. A few were adults, and seeing these kites up close, with their gray head feathers and thin black masks, their small black beaks and intelligent red eyes, was fascinating, though bittersweet. While I was grateful for this opportunity, I was also saddened by their injuries. They were receiving excellent care, however, and Rondi told us they would soon be released in time to make their autumn migrations to South America.

Indeed, it is in the air where the Mississippi kite's inherent beauty and grace, of which the Baumgartners wrote in *Oklahoma Bird Life*, are most apparent, for when taking to the sky these seemingly pigeon-sized birds suddenly become much larger, and even more elegant. The difference is in their wings, which reach three feet when fully extended. They're not the rounded, heavy wings of a hawk or an eagle; the Mississippi kite's wings are long and slender. Kites, like falcons, have pointed wings and long tails. But whereas falcons are powerful fliers, kites use their wings to glide easily and gracefully through our skies.

The eighteenth-century botanist William Bartram noted these wings in his description of the kite in his celebrated book *Travels* (1791). "Kite hawks," he writes, "are characterized by having long sharp pointed wings, being of swift flight, sailing without flapping their wings, lean light bodies, and feeding out of their claws on the wing, as they gently sail round and round." In his list of these birds, he included a *Falco subceruleus*, describing it as "the sharp winged hawk, of a dark or dusky blue colour." One wonders whether the author was referring specifically to the Mississippi kite or to another species. We'll probably never know. After all, *Travels* is based on Bartram's experiences visiting the southeastern United States, especially the Carolinas, Georgia, and Florida, the latter a state where even today one can view four species of kites, including the snail kite (also known as the Everglades kite) as well as the white-tailed, swallow-tailed, and Mississippi kites.

Regardless of whether Bartram's *"Falco subceruleus"* was in reference to the Mississippi kite specifically or another species, his use of the term "kite hawk" was nevertheless revolutionary according to authors Eric G. Bolen and Dan Flores, who note in their book *The Mississippi Kite* (1993) that "Bartram seems to have been the first American naturalist to use the term *kite*."

Interestingly, the Reverend Gilbert White, an Englishman, used the same word to describe these birds in *The Natural History of Selborne* (1789), published two years before Bartram's *Travels*. In White's August 7, 1778, letter to naturalist Daines Barrington, he points out that there is something peculiar to many birds "that at first sight discriminates them, and enables a judicious observer to pronounce upon them with some certainty." The first birds White then mentions are kites, which "sail round in circles with wings expanded and motionless."

Clearly, at the time of the American Revolution, naturalists on both sides of the Atlantic were using the term "kite" in describing these distinguished raptors, which likely reflected a long history of such use, especially in Europe. In fact, Swedish naturalist Carl Linnaeus included the red kite, a European species, in the tenth edition of his *Systema Naturae* (1758), categorizing it with the binomial *Falcus milvus*, the latter from the Latin for "kite."

According to Diana Wells, author of *100 Birds and How They Got Their Names* (2001), the name "kite" goes back even farther and is derived from the Anglo-Saxon *cyta*, from *skut*, meaning to "swoop."

But what of the other type of kites, the tethered flying instruments? They were well known in Europe, having been used there for centuries, and in Asia for millennia. These devices are believed to have originated in China over two thousand years ago, although some contend that kites were also being used in the South Pacific during this time for fishing. According to legend, the ancient Chinese philosopher Mozi (470–391 B.C.) spent three years developing the world's first kite, a "wooden bird" that took the form of a sparrow hawk and was destroyed in a fall on its very first day in flight. Evidently inspired by this success, and perhaps feeling the wind beneath his own wings, Mozi's student Lu Ban later improved on this design with a kite built of bamboo and silk, which he is said to have flown continuously for three days.

The Cornell Lab of Ornithology notes that kites, like many modern birds, diverged from the more ancient lineages of Aves sometime around two million years ago. Which means that these graceful raptors had been soaring the world's skies for ages at the relatively recent time Mozi and Lu Ban were experimenting with the world's first tethered flying instruments.

Like the bird, like the tethered flying instrument, the term "kite" has proven both adaptable and versatile. It has even expanded its traditional range. According to the *Merriam-Webster Dictionary*, "kite" can be used to describe (a) "any of various usually small hawks (family Accipitridae) with long narrow wings and often a notched or forked tail," or (b) a light frame covered with cloth, paper, or plastic, designed to be flown in the air at the end of a string, as well as (c) a person who preys on others, or (d) a light sail used in calm conditions in addition to a vessel's regular working sails.

In the world of geometry, a "kite" is a quadrilateral with two distinct pairs of congruent, adjacent sides. The word is also used as a verb, meaning to move or fly easily, like a kite, or to obtain money or credit through a deceptive process known in banking (and law enforcement) as "kiting," which refers to the act of passing checks drawn on uncollected funds in a bank account. In the days before debit cards and automatic teller machines (ATMs), kiting checks was a real problem, and as someone who once worked in a bank, I recall that it often resulted in a very specific request from certain businesses: "Does this bank do skip-tracing?"

Perhaps not surprisingly, the *Merriam-Webster Dictionary* also recognizes the word "kitelike," although I've not had the privilege to hear this adjective uttered publicly. Beyond the field of hang gliding, I can't imagine a situation to which it would aptly apply, for while I've heard others use the term "catlike" to describe certain furtive behaviors or especially acrobatic athletes or circus perform-ers, I am still waiting, with bated breath, to hear someone utter, "That dude was so kitelike, the way he went up and soared over everyone else . . . and grabbed the ball with his feet!"

III. THREATS

These beautiful and beneficial birds should be
protected by every means in our power.
    —MARGARET MORSE NICE, *The Birds of Oklahoma*

The American ethologist and ornithologist Margaret Morse Nice was unknown to me until fairly recently. I learned about her while researching Mississippi kites and was fascinated to discover that she'd published a book dedicated to the close study of Oklahoma's avifauna: *The Birds of Oklahoma* (1924), which was revised in 1931. Born in Massachusetts in 1883, Nice developed an interest in nature at an early age, and she earned a master's degree in zoology from Clark University, writing her thesis on the eating habits of the northern bobwhite (*Colinus virginianus*).

In 1913, Nice's husband, Leonard Blaine Nice, accepted a posi-tion in the department of physiology at the University of Oklahoma, and the couple relocated to Norman. While living in Oklahoma, Margaret's appreciation for nature was rekindled and she began a close study of the area's birds. This research was the basis for her book *The Birds of Oklahoma*.

Margaret Morse Nice eventually wrote seven books and gained international recognition for her landmark two-volume work

Studies in the Life History of the Song Sparrow (1937 and 1943). Aldo Leopold recognized her in *A Sand County Almanac* while referencing the increasing value of amateur research for fields such as biology. "Margaret Morse Nice, an amateur ornithologist, studied song sparrows in her backyard," he writes. "She has become a world-authority on bird behavior, and has outthought and outworked many a professional student of social organization in birds."

Indeed, Nice's dedication to her ornithological work is inspiring, and it's one of the reasons why *The Birds of Oklahoma* is so intriguing, particularly the 1931 revised edition, which reflects a considerable amount of field research by Nice herself, as well as avifauna-related observations by many earlier visitors to the southern Great Plains, such as S. W. Woodhouse, Thomas Nuttall, Randolph Marcy, and others. And I admire Mrs. Nice's willingness to take a stand on the issue of feral and domestic free-roaming cats, which regrettably kill more than *one billion* wild birds in the United States each year, according to the Smithsonian Conservation Biology Institute. (Felines are so problematic that the International Union for Conservation of Nature includes house cats on its list of the world's one hundred worst invasive species, along with the European starling, zebra mussels, and Asian tiger mosquito.)

Cats, however, aren't typically included among the most common threats to Mississippi kites. Perhaps this is due to the kite's proclivity for constructing nests higher in trees than some other birds, the latter of which may present easier opportunities for felines and other land-based predators, or maybe it's a result of the Mississippi kite's vigorous defense of the nest. For kites, much more pressing threats are the great horned owl, and especially our use of pesticides that find their way into the food chain, as well as habitat loss resulting from suburban and exurban sprawl.

In addition to the Mississippi kite, two additional kites were once found, one apparently in limited numbers, in Oklahoma.

S. W. Woodhouse, who visited Indian Territory from 1849 to 1850, described the swallow-tailed kite as "common" in Texas and in the Creek and Cherokee Nations and called it "very abundant" along the Arkansas River and its tributaries.

In *The Birds of Oklahoma*, Nice noted that this species was "formerly a common summer resident," which hasn't been recorded in the state since 1910.

Similarly, the white-tailed kite, once a "rare summer resident," had disappeared from the state at the time Nice wrote *The Birds of Oklahoma*. Why? What happened? In short, European settlement and unregulated development of a formerly pristine landscape. The seventy-five-year period between Woodhouse's visit and the publication of Nice's book in 1924 was a pivotal time that saw an enormous influx of settlers to the region, as well as unprecedented (for Indian Territory) development and natural habitat destruction. Much of this seventy-five-year period was also an era of unregulated hunting and trapping, which resulted in the extirpation of numerous species from the region, such as bears, mountain lions, and wolves. It was during this period that the heartless slaughter of American bison by white "hunters" pushed this magnificent animal to the brink of extinction. It was also a time that saw the passenger pigeon—the "finest of all pigeons," according to Margaret Morse Nice, once exceedingly common in eastern Oklahoma—eradicated from our planet, never to return again. About this, Mrs. Nice wrote, "there is no blacker page in American history."

It was certainly with all this and more in mind that Mrs. Nice cautioned her readers to make every effort to protect the Mississippi kite. While the bird has proven adaptable, having found central and western Oklahoma, and even some of our urban areas, to its liking, its cousin the snail kite is having a tough time of it in South Florida. Though the snail kite is widespread across Central and South

America, in the United States it's considered endangered because of the ongoing degradation of its native Everglades habitat.

The same could be said of our Mississippi kite if (a) we can't find a way to curtail our tendency to destroy natural habitat, especially mature trees; or (b) we fail to preserve our riparian buffers, which are so important for kites and scores of other species, as well as the health of our creeks, streams, and rivers; or (c) we fail to properly manage our use of pesticides. In this sense, perhaps it's to the Mississippi kite's benefit that it is here with us for only part of the year.

IV. FIELD NOTES

> Men that undertake only one district are much more
> likely to advance natural knowledge than those that
> grasp at more than they can possibly be acquainted
> with: every kingdom, every province, should have its
> own monographer.
>
> —GILBERT WHITE, *The Natural History of Selborne*

Reasoning that I would have had Gilbert White's support and encouragement had he been here to support and encourage me, and finding myself so intrigued by Mississippi kites that I felt compelled to observe them at every opportunity and to note something about them each time I stepped outdoors, I decided to record the kites' autumn 2016 departure from my neighborhood in northern Oklahoma County, which commenced, according to my observations, on August 20. For the next month I noted a steady stream of Mississippi kites moving through the area, which continued until September 19. This marked the last day I sighted the birds in my neighborhood.

While I'm not suggesting that these observations are going to have much of an impact in advancing natural knowledge as White posited, I note them here simply because I found the birds' habits interesting, and because these notes will serve as a starting point for future study, which, with time, should certainly reveal more about them.

I awoke this morning to find that yesterday's tempestuous winds had calmed, and that our kites were gone. Yesterday, all week in fact, they'd been very active as they glided across the sky, spiraling high on rising thermals, whirling, wheeling, speeding by with the wind.

As I jogged through the neighborhood one day last week, I spotted a kite circling above a nearby house. Upon seeing me the bird glided over and seemed to soar above me for a while. Kites once followed buffalo as they moved through the tall plains grasses, stirring insects into the air, so I suppose they're instinctively driven to do this, even if their flushing dog isn't a bison but a gasping, struggling, sweaty human. I watched the kite's shadow on the street pavement as it shadowed me for a short distance before tilting its wings and veering away with the wind. I felt fortunate that it seemed to have acknowledged me. I only wish that I had its eyesight and agility.

All week the weather had been strange, with high temps averaging ten degrees or more cooler than usual. Friday was windy, with alternating clouds and sun, and high temps only in the seventies. Large, dark clouds moved in several times that afternoon. I thought we'd get rain, but we didn't. The kites were very active on this day, kettling high in the sky to help the younger birds build their endurance for their long flights. For the past several weeks I'd been telling Jackson the kites would soon be leaving us. I didn't know today would be the day.

The winds subsided Friday evening, and when we woke up on Saturday the air was cool, conditions calm, and the kites gone. I looked all over, including among the dead treetop branches on which they often perched, the nearby power lines, everywhere I could think of. Nothing. At one point in the day I saw buzzards circling high overhead, but no kites.

Driving home Saturday afternoon, passing along a section of road where several times that summer I'd seen a kite perched on a certain section of power line, I spotted one of the birds flying above me. It was some relief to know not all of them had left in advance of the approaching front. Winds today were gentle and out of the northwest, skies mostly sunny with some clouds, and temps reached into the eighties. I know that soon even this kite, and all the others, will migrate south for the winter and we won't see them again until next spring. It makes me sad. After watching them all summer, seeing them every time I went outside, I feel they've become high-altitude companions of mine, and the skies seem incredibly empty now.

AUGUST 21, 2016

This morning dawned calm and cool, with the promise of sunny skies and warm afternoon temperatures. And on a midmorning walk with the dogs, I noticed a kite! Now two of them! And now three! Were these the same kites that had been with us all summer? Or were they new kites, having moved down from northern Oklahoma in advance of the cool weather we were now feeling? It was impossible to tell, but I was inclined to believe they were new arrivals for the simple fact that they were flying at some considerable altitude at an early hour—a time at which, all summer long, our local kites flew only fifty or one hundred feet above the ground, and often lower, just over the treetops. Of course, I have no way of knowing.

As I jogged late this morning, I spotted many kites soaring above the neighborhood, witnessing one bird's swift descent in which it swooped quite low in pursuit of some unseen insect before ascending into the sky once again. Someone was baking a spice cake, which filled the air out on the street with a wonderful aroma. Savoring this sweet scent, feeling the cooler air, the quiet and languorous Sunday atmosphere, I thought it seemed very much an autumn, rather than late-summer, day.

Late in the afternoon I took my binoculars to the swimming pool and stood there watching kites all around me, soaring so gracefully in the sky—an impossibly blue sky, clear with only a few light, wispy clouds. I watched as they glided by with wings spread wide, perfectly extended, and now and then folding only their wing tips in to swoop or dive. As they soared, I noticed that their tails resembled pie-shaped wedges, and that they were constantly moving, tilting to the left, to the right, always shifting to the birds' desires. It was enjoyable to watch these adult kites glide through the sky so easily and effortlessly, their gray heads looking left, right, and below as they scanned for insects. I watched one kite fold in its wings and swoop down to catch a bug in much the same trajectory as a roller coaster dips and dives before ascending the next hill. One kite, I noticed, had a large insect, probably a cicada or dragonfly, in its beak as it flew. Though conditions were calm on the ground, I could tell the wind had some velocity a hundred feet above, for the kites, when spinning around and wheeling with the wind, would glide most rapidly across the sky before turning again and spiraling higher and higher, as if scouring the inside of some transparent cereal bowl.

Today must have been the nicest, most pleasant day of the entire year. Conditions were sunny and calm, with afternoon temperatures hovering in the mideighties. Seeing so many kites flying through the sky was a big reason why. Even if they depart for their winter grounds tomorrow, we've had this day with them, and what a day it was!

AUGUST 22, 2016

Cool this morning. Cool enough that I pulled on a long-sleeved shirt as I sat down at my desk to work. Later, it warmed into the eighties and as I ran I spotted nine kites! It took a while; I didn't see any for the first half of my run. Then I began to notice birds soaring over rooftops, gliding high, sweeping with the wind across the sky. I delighted in hearing their *Phee, phew!* calls, from both airborne birds and even perched kites.

The birds I've seen lately have varied greatly in number. One day the skies are full of kites, and the next I may see only a few, followed by more the following day (though not as many as the first day), and so on. I wonder: What does a kite look for when deciding when to embark on its remarkably long and difficult flight to South America? Does it gaze into the eyes of a friend, neighbor, or companion and decide there and then that the time to fly has arrived? Or does it simply turn wing at the first brush of cool or unsettled weather and let the wind carry it so effortlessly and gracefully across the sky as it makes for southern climes?

This evening I spotted two kites, including a juvenile, flying around our church in Oklahoma City. The young kite called repeatedly from its cypress-tree perch. *Phee, phew! Phee, phew!* Then it would fly off, circling above the church for a short while before returning to the tree where, at 7:45 P.M., it seemed to go to roost. I never saw it leave the tree again after this time.

There are not as many kites here in the city as around my house on the outskirts of town. Nevertheless, I'm happy to see these birds, and the fact that they can make a living here in the city showcases their adaptability.

AUGUST 23, 2016

As I've been busy with work this morning, I haven't been out much today, only once to walk my dogs. While we were out, I saw two kites soaring low over a rooftop, and another that seemed to hover in the air as the strong breeze pushed it sideways very much like a wind-buffeted helicopter hovering over some incident on the ground, but more easily and quickly restored to its former position, and so much more beautiful.

Sitting here at my desk this morning, I twice heard the *Phee, phew!* of a Mississippi kite. What a delight!

AUGUST 24, 2016

Summer has returned in full force. Temperatures reached into the nineties yesterday afternoon, and by midmorning today the sun had a bite to it. Very windy the past two days, and this has made for some enjoyable kite viewing. I've spotted kites hovering in the sky, almost motionless, as they utilize the wind to help maintain position while they scan the airspace below. Like a free-falling skydiver, or those Southern California hang gliders, the kites, with wings spread wide, make only the slightest movements to adjust their position, to veer up or down or left or right. They use the wind to their advantage to expend as little effort and energy as possible. They're incredibly grateful, these elegant, slender kites.

While out on my morning run, I saw a juvenile kite flying low, just over the treetops along the creek, and noticed its beautiful barred underside, its powerful legs folded back in aerodynamic fashion, pie-wedge-shaped tail in constant motion, canting left and right to keep the bird in the desired position. While I have no way of knowing for sure, being unable to measure one of the birds myself, it seems the Mississippi kite's wingspan, which can reach three feet, is three times the length of its body. Perhaps a bit more.

Yesterday I noticed a kite and buzzard gliding through the

air in the same vicinity, but at different altitudes. The buzzard appeared to fly some twenty feet or more higher than the kite. It was also much larger. At one point, the kite circled and veered close to the buzzard, which seemed not to notice or care, and then the kite wheeled and shot away with the wind.

AUGUST 25, 2016

Another sunny, hot morning. Today I heard the *Phee, phew!* of a kite, though I couldn't locate the bird. While I was running up a long hill, movement to my left caught my attention. I looked to see a kite's perfect shadow gliding across the roof of a nearby house. Up it went, nearly to the peak, before turning and gliding back down the roof, where it disappeared. Near the end of my run, I spotted a kite soaring above the trees along the creek. It was flying away from me, and suddenly it turned and headed back, passing overhead just as I finished my run, then disappearing behind the screen of trees.

Later in the afternoon, as clouds were building in the north, I spotted a couple of gliding kites, carving spirals high in the sky with one of these large, white cumulonimbus clouds as a backdrop. They reminded me of eagles flying across a snow-covered mountain range.

The songbirds are no longer singing in the mornings, or any time of day. Even the mockingbirds are silent now, for the first time since spring. I saw one on a rooftop yesterday and it just sat there, silently looking out over the neighborhood. I'm seeing fewer cardinals, too. Soon, they'll confine themselves to the thickets and shrubs and woods, where they'll molt, exchanging this year's feathers for a new set, and we won't see much of them again until this winter, when they'll join flocks of other cardinals and frequent our backyard feeders. About this flocking phenomenon, whereby birds group together during periods of cold, inclement weather, which ornithologists typically attribute to a safety precaution—more eyes make it easier to spot potential predators, thus helping keep the flock safe—Gilbert White had some thoughts, likening this habit to groups of men gravitating to one another when sharing some common adversity. "As some kind of self-interest and self-defence is no doubt the motive for the proceeding, may it not arise from the helplessness of their state in such rigorous seasons; as men crowd together, when under great calamities, though they know why not?"

With our songbirds seemingly at the cusp of their "off-season," the kites are increasingly a source of pleasure and wonder, and every time I go outside I look up into the sky in hopes of spotting one, knowing that the kites, too, are soon to leave us until next year.

Today while jogging I saw a roadrunner running across the street ahead of me. When it spotted me, it picked up the pace and ran into a yard at a surprisingly high rate of speed. These birds can move! But as I continued to approach the bird's general direction, it apparently decided that it wanted to put more space between us, so it simultaneously jumped and flapped its wings, with the result that the roadrunner flew onto the roof of the nearest house. Not only this, but it landed on the peak of this very tall roof, where it stood watching me as I jogged by. I have seen roadrunners fly for short distances close to the ground, as a chicken might, but I'd never seen one of these heavy-bodied, land-oriented sprinters attain such a considerable height, and with such ease. I've often thought that roadrunners are formidable predators. These athletic birds are so capable and perfectly adapted to locate, pursue, capture, and subdue their prey.

AUGUST 26, 2016

Some mornings, when I really should be writing, I sit instead at the computer with my coffee, looking out the windows into my backyard and our thin strip of forest. Usually, there are birds flitting about the trees, or squirrels racing through the branches. In November, as the vegetation thins, I often see deer darting back and forth in the field across the creek. Sometimes I take my coffee, walk to the front of the house, and stand staring out at the street to see, I suppose, what's going on, who's walking or driving by, and whether there are any birds in my front yard. By now, most of my neighbors have left for work. The first school bus, the one for the older kids, has come and gone. And the morning dog walkers have already walked their dogs. Whereas in the spring or early summer I could count on spotting a mockingbird, some robins, or a pair of doves policing my front yard for a worm or cricket, now it's empty. The grass, while still green, has a brown spot—I refuse to give it enough water to keep it green, simply because this is a poor use of our precious water; besides, the entire lawn will soon be going dormant, which means even our greenest, most hydrated yards will be turning brown—although I notice, with some disappointment, that my holly bushes need to be trimmed again, even though I did this just last week. Now comes the police officer who lives up the street, riding his BMW motorcycle as he leaves for a day at work. Or is he already there, now that he's suited up in uniform and riding his city beat?

This morning at 7:43 I was doing exactly this, and I happened to look up into the calm blue sky above my neighbors' houses—the confined block of sky that I can see from my front door—and I spotted a kite flying across this small window, flapping its wings as it headed south, then pausing for a moment, gliding in full profile, and then again flapping its wings before disappearing from view. Total time spent looking out the front door: less than a minute. But you know it's going to be a good day when you spot a kite from inside your home first thing in the morning. Plus, it's Friday.

Midmorning, after taking my son to school, I noticed an

intense concentration of kites, about ten of them, kettling above a wooded area directly across the street from a new housing development. Much cooler this morning. Temperature at 9:30 A.M. was only seventy-four degrees, with gentle north winds.

While walking the dogs at lunchtime, I came upon a juvenile kite perched on a river birch's topmost branch. I walked beneath the tree and the bird remained on its post. Then, when I stopped, I heard a distant kite call and the juvenile in the tree above me took to the sky, flapping its wings as it disappeared behind the houses across the street. As it flew off, the young kite called *Phee, phew!* in a rather scratchy tone.

I saw a similar type of behavior earlier this summer in Florida, when a mother mockingbird, perched in a live-oak tree, called to her fledgling on the ground. Up to this point, the mother had been scrambling to feed the hungry young bird, which was noisily protesting the wait times between meals. She would deliver a worm or some insect, and before she could fly away the fledgling would consume the morsel and begin crying for more. At one point, while the mother was away hunting for food, an adult brown thrasher, scratching through the leaves nearby, moved over and pecked the young mockingbird on the head as if to say, *Stop this fussing! Your mother is doing the best she can!* A few minutes later, the mother returned with a worm, but before she could fly off, the younger bird began one of these outbursts. The harried mother mockingbird seemed to have had enough. There was a quick rustling of feathers, a sharp peck to the head, and the mother flew away. At this point, the grounded fledgling crouched in place and sat motionless and silent until, upon hearing its mother's call some ten minutes later, it flew instantly and directly to the tree where she waited.

Kites filled the sky this afternoon, some low, just over the rooftops, while others were gliding very high up. I noticed a couple of buzzards, much larger than the kites and flying at a higher altitude. They never appear aggressive toward the smaller birds, though their larger size makes me wonder whether they might behave this way. The kites seem to show no concern and simply go about their day.

Regarding the kite's call, lately, especially today, I've noticed it sounds slightly sharper than I'm used to hearing. Normally, it's *Phee, phew!* with a slight emphasis on the beginning of the second syllable before the sound slowly trails off. Phee, *phew!* Today it sounded just a bit quicker and sharper, with the stress on the first syllable: *Phee*, phew! The sound of the second syllable trails off as before, but there seems to be more emphasis on the first sharp note. Is this a call made from an adult to a juvenile kite? I wonder, given my earlier observation of the younger bird perched on the river birch.

Whenever I hear this call, I'm grateful I'm not driving on some noisy, foul-smelling interstate, or trapped in a concrete-encased city, and thus deprived of the glorious natural world. I'm grateful that I can hear the kite's call, because if I were sealed inside a car, or astride a raucous motorcycle, I wouldn't hear it at all.

AUGUST 27, 2016
I saw only one kite today, a distant silhouette gliding against the backdrop of a large white cloud looming over a busy Oklahoma highway.

AUGUST 28, 2016
One kite today: a juvenile, perched on a roadside power line. Where have all the kites gone?

AUGUST 29, 2016
My wife tells me she saw a dozen or more kites this morning while driving my son to school. Things are looking up!

And yet while I was out this afternoon, the skies were empty of these birds. Though I heard the call, I sighted only one: a juvenile atop a creek-side oak, sitting in the sun.

AUGUST 30, 2016

No kites in sight this morning, nor have I heard any calling. I have, however, heard several red-tailed hawks calling the past two days. Lots of tropical moisture in the atmosphere now. Yesterday afternoon we had a very brief but intense rain shower—something a local meteorologist said was repeated across the southern plains yesterday, and possibly would be again the next two days. Recent weather pattern: sunny and calm mornings with clouds building in early afternoon; brief rain showers or possibility thereof, accompanied by strong winds, in midafternoon; clearing somewhat by evening. Temps warm (high eighties or low nineties) and about ten degrees cooler than usual.

Yesterday morning I spotted a redbud leaf on my front porch, which had fallen from the tree in my flowerbed. It contained two beads of water, one quarter-sized and the other the size of a nickel. Interestingly, these beads remained on the leaf throughout the day, never dissipating, never blowing away in the strong winds heralding the afternoon rain. The beads were rather flat, and at one point, owing to the light I suppose, they began to resemble a dollop of epoxy rather than a perfect bubble of water, so I touched one, the largest, just to see how it felt. It was warm, and it jiggled slightly without breaking up or sliding off the leaf. Jiggled. Quivered. Quavered. This suggests the water beads maintained some surface tension against the redbud leaf. I would have expected them to move more easily, more freely, across the leaf. Most remarkably, these beads seemed to remain the same size all day, despite the afternoon heat.

This morning when I looked out, the smaller of the two beads had dried up in the night, while the larger bead remained much as it had yesterday—flat and semiopaque, although this could be the result of it resting on the green redbud leaf, which prevents light from passing through the bead and illuminating it like a miniature house of mirrors, reflecting its transparency.

The redbud leaf is insulating the water bead from the very warm brick pavers on which it rests; otherwise it would have already evaporated.

Around noon I went out for a walk and noticed an isolated kite flying high overhead. Some distance away, I noticed another, this one calling *Phee, phew!* and at one point folding in its wing tips and swooping down on an insect, evidently, before looping back to its former altitude. Lots of buzzards about, flying very high, well above the few kites I'm seeing. Heard a red-tailed hawk screaming from somewhere nearby, and saw a great blue heron pumping its wings as it flew low and close to the creek. Sunny skies with clouds building to the north and west.

Clouds passing in front of the sun at 2:00 P.M., dimming the ambient light, then drifting off and the skies brightening again. Going out to check the mail, I noticed the redbud leaf was dry and brittle now, whereas yesterday morning it had been soft and pliant. The quarter-sized drop of water was still holding strong. When I tilted the leaf, the water bead moved freely and easily, exhibiting less surface tension against the leaf than before. Somewhat like the creek, which is flowing vigorously after yesterday's downpour.

With things slowing down in my area, I contacted WildCare, the nonprofit wildlife rehabilitation center east of Noble, Oklahoma, to ask whether they were receiving any kites. I expected that they might have a bird or two. They had forty kites, thirty-six of which were juveniles. I hadn't expected so many, but the staff assured me this was nothing compared to the drought year of 2010, when conditions were so hot that nestlings were jumping out of their sizzling treetop homes before they could fly. That year, three hundred kites were brought to WildCare for treatment!

This afternoon, a ranger at the Wichita Mountains Wildlife Refuge emailed me to say he'd seen a Mississippi kite yesterday near the refuge's prairie dog town, adding that a few of these birds were still around.

AUGUST 31, 2016

The last day of August, and as far as I'm concerned, the last real day of summer. It's a sad day. This summer has been a good one, and I hate to see it go. I am no fan of cool weather. I love the heat, the sunshine. I wish I could pack up and head south with the kites.

This morning I saw eight kites kettling at a very high altitude above my neighborhood—much higher than they normally fly. I might have missed seeing them if not for the faint *Phee, phew!* that met my ears like the voice of an old friend saying hi.

Spotted a lone kite gliding low over the busy interstate at about 9:30 this morning, flying toward a grove of cottonwood trees.

The bead of water on my front porch has evaporated, leaving only a faint outline of its former existence on the shriveled redbud leaf, which the wind will soon carry away as if it never existed.

Late this morning, while running, I heard kites calling from high in the sky, but I never saw them. It was as if the birds were watching over me as I ran, their summer spirits keeping me energized and positive with the coming of autumn, telling me that they'll be back next year.

This evening, at the invitation of Rondi Large, Jackson and I visited WildCare to view the Mississippi kites they'd taken in. With the migration underway, I wanted to know how soon these birds would be released, and whether they could fly right away. To our surprise, Rondi told me her staff had released ten juvenile kites ("kids," as she called them) earlier in the day, and while leading us to the kite enclosure on her property, she pointed to a couple of the beautiful birds perched on a nearby oak tree.

"They generally hang around for a while," Rondi said. "They're used to us feeding them. We try to keep food out to assist the kids as they learn how feed themselves."

Food for kites is predominantly insects, especially dragonflies, cicadas, crickets, beetles, and grasshoppers. Rondi said at this time of year the kites follow the dragonflies as they move south.

While in the care of Rondi and her staff, the kites are fed a commercial food mixture that helps them recover from their injuries, most of which are, regrettably, caused by humans.

"I used to wonder how a golfer could hit a kite with a golf ball," Rondi said. "I eventually learned they don't. They swing at them with their clubs when the kites swoop down to defend their nests."

It tore my heart in two to hear this, to learn of yet another way society is taking its toll on wildlife. These birds, however, were in good hands. Rondi showed us an adult kite with a broken wing. It had a bandage wrapped around its body. Another, which was nearly fully recovered from a wing injury, hissed at us as we opened the cage door and peered in.

The adults are naturally, and wisely, fearful of humans, something Rondi said the kids haven't yet learned, and which I witnessed firsthand as I entered the juvenile kites' enclosure. Inside, there were perhaps a dozen young kites, all of which had been born earlier this summer. Unlike the adults, with their smooth gray head feathers and dark backs and wings, these young kites had barred feathers in shades of white, black, and gray. They were beautiful birds. They were about the size of a pigeon, but of course with a much larger wingspan and that unmistakably athletic raptor physique. They were extremely calm and observant, never showing any signs of fear or discomfort as they watched me photographing them from only a few feet away. Rondi said these birds are hand-fed daily, and I wished it had been feeding time.

Mississippi kites don't tolerate cold, rainy weather and are typically among the first raptors to begin their fall migrations. For this reason, Rondi told me, her staff was working to release the birds as quickly as possible. This begins with what she calls a "soft release," whereby the kites are turned loose, although many often choose to remain nearby. Eventually, these young birds will join migrating kettles of kites for their long journey to South America.

At the time of our visit, WildCare had taken in 144 kites for the year, with the first bird having come in on May 3. While this figure is significant, it's less than half the number of kites brought in during the severe drought years of 2010–2011. "Most of these were kids, nestlings and fledglings jumping out of the nest before they could fly," Rondi said. "When it's so hot and dry, it might be a hundred and ten degrees in the nest. They were just seeking relief from the extreme heat."

Fortunately, 2016 has been a most unusual summer for Oklahoma, with consistent rainfall and mild temperatures, seldom exceeding one hundred degrees.

Just before leaving, we stopped at another kite enclosure and observed the "kids" inside. Two of the kites began whining when they saw us. They sounded like puppies.

"They think we're going to feed them," Rondi said.

Another, perched nearby, opened up its little black beak and called out that familiar *Phee, phew!* It made me smile, for all summer long I'd heard that same sweet song.

SEPTEMBER 6, 2016

There are still a few kites around central Oklahoma. In my neighborhood, each of the past three days I've heard a juvenile kite calling from a certain oak tree situated along our creek. The young bird has lately been perched at the top of this tree while an adult kite circles the skies nearby, hunting for food, which it then delivers to the youngster. This morning I watched the adult make a dramatic descent of perhaps one hundred feet, a dive in which it swooped down between two houses before looping back toward the sky and then gliding gently to the tree where its hungry offspring was waiting. The young bird had been calling, and when it spotted its parent bringing it food it began whining. The busy provider alighted on the branch beside the young kite, delivered the food, and then flew away two seconds later.

In the past few days, an opening has appeared in the foliage of the sweetgum tree where, way back in May, I saw one of the year's first kites. This aperture has allowed me to see the kite's nest, which is situated perhaps forty feet above the ground and fifteen feet below the top of the tree. The nest is the size of a very large dinner plate. It is flat, not more than a few inches in height, and constructed of sticks and twigs roughly the diameter of pencils.

The oak tree on which I've seen the juvenile kite perched the last few days is just across the street from this sweetgum. Probably, there are several more nests in the vicinity, hidden by the green foliage.

Lots of dragonflies in the air right now. The fall webworms have absolutely inundated the black walnut trees along our creek. The scions of these trees are covered in hazy gray webs and are defoliated, exposing the developing walnuts hanging from their limbs. I'm sure the birds are enjoying this sudden bounty. I wonder whether the kites eat these webworm larvae.

The past two mornings the owls have begun hooting around 4:30, well before sunrise, and have kept it up very rhythmically, calling every eight seconds, until 6:30 A.M., when they seem to vanish. Every time I hear the owls hooting in the still, predawn darkness, I'm reminded of Washington Irving's book *A Tour on the Prairies*, in which the author documents, again and again, the competence and wisdom displayed by his French Osage guide, Pierre Beatte, as they explored the wild frontier lands of Indian Territory in the autumn of 1832. As their party lay in their bedrolls in the predawn darkness early one morning, Beatte remarked that dawn wasn't far off, for he'd just heard an owl hoot. Irving then asked Beatte whether owls always hoot before daybreak, and the latter replied, "Aye, sir, just as the cock crows."

SEPTEMBER 7, 2016

Saw only one kite this morning. It was a young bird perched on a power line. Weather: windy, cloudy, and warm with a chance of rain. In the afternoon, I noticed a kite soaring over our creek, and another gliding through the skies near my son's school in Oklahoma City.

SEPTEMBER 9, 2016

At 9:00 A.M. a juvenile kite was on the usual perch at the "feeding tree" along our creek. It appeared to be picking at remnants of a meal, and upon noticing a mockingbird nearby, it let out a sharp *Phee, phew!* and the mocker retreated, flying to another branch. This occurred several times, at one point attracting another mockingbird. When they would approach too closely, the young kite would dip its head in a defensive (or aggressive?) posture and the mockingbirds would retreat. This went on for about five minutes, during which time the kite was silent. Then it began calling steadily, and I knew its parent was approaching. A moment later, the adult bird flew up and attempted to deliver a meal beak to beak, but the younger bird failed to grasp the food item. Without ever landing, the adult flew to another limb. The young kite followed, flapping its wings and "whining" like a puppy. Is the adult testing the juvenile? When this young bird is alone it appears entirely self-sufficient and confident. Yet at the sight of its parent approaching, the young kite becomes excited and begins calling repeatedly, the call soon becoming a constant, high-pitched whining. If you were blind-folded and couldn't view the interaction between these kites, you could follow it through the young bird's calls and excited whining.

An hour or so later, I heard a kite calling from a sweetgum tree (the one in which I recently spotted the nest) across the street from our creek. I noticed a juvenile kite perched on a limb just above this nest, watching me and calling regularly, *Phee, phew!* It's interesting that at this late date the kites—this kite, at least—are so oriented toward the nest.

The fall webworms are all over my back porch, and I spotted a web of them at the base of the redbud tree I planted in the corner of our backyard. The black walnut trees along our creek are so infested with them that they appear to be smoldering, the gray, gauzy webs suggesting so many clouds of smoke. For the past two weeks I've noticed lots of blue jays around the neighborhood, squawking noisily in the trees. I wonder whether they're eating these webworm larvae.

SEPTEMBER 10, 2016

Cooler this morning after thunderstorms last night. Sunny, warm, calm day—beautiful. The juvenile kite was in the "feeding tree" along the creek this morning. I did not notice the adult, which has been delivering food. There were several red-tailed hawks around. I heard them calling from the air. A large female redtail perched on a nearby elm tree. The young kite did not appear to notice the hawk until the latter flew off, at which point the juvenile kite, apparently believing this large bird to be his parent, called one time. The hawk paid no attention and disappeared. This young kite appears to be a second-year bird. It has the light gray head of an adult, yet I'm not sure why it's reliant on its parents for food. All the other kites in my neighborhood have gone.

SEPTEMBER 12, 2016

Warmer today. At 10:00 A.M. I spotted two kites gliding above the trees along my creek. An hour or so later, while returning from my run, I heard a kite calling and watched this bird for a minute or more as it circled, soaring higher and higher until it suddenly and very smoothly, effortlessly, inverted and went into a swift dive, and then momentarily disappeared behind a screen of trees, reappearing moments later on the other side of the creek. I know fighter pilots perform such maneuvers, but even the best ace who ever flew wasn't half as graceful or as swift and elegant as this beautiful Mississippi kite, which then flew to the sweetgum tree where a juvenile kite was calling. Despite the heavy foliage on the tree, this young kite began calling repeatedly when it spotted the adult approaching. I was surprised the young bird could see through all the foliage, but this proved no barrier for the juvenile, or the parent, which slipped into the tree, delivered the meal, and flew off again. I watched the young kite eating in the nest. Afterward, it hopped up on the branch just above the nest and began calling as before. Two minutes later, the adult kite returned and the process was repeated.

Sunny and warm today, with gusty south winds.

SEPTEMBER 14, 2016

Cooler this morning with rain. No sign of the kites all day.

SEPTEMBER 15, 2016

Saw two kites this morning flying over the creek, headed northwest. Around 9:30 A.M., while walking the dogs, I heard and then saw a juvenile kite calling from the feeding tree along the creek. Adult kite brought food, evidently passed it to juvenile, and then flew away a second later, and yet the juvenile continued calling for several seconds. Was the food dropped? Did the adult tease the young bird with a morsel of food to get it to fly, move, jump? Did it eat the food that quickly? Or does the young kite call like this more from the sight of its parent than out of hunger? It's a large bird, as large as kites get, though still in the dark, juvenile plumage.

That the adult kite is ranging farther and farther for food was evident in the nearly ten minutes that passed before it returned to the feeding tree. Formerly, I've noticed adult kites returning every two minutes. This suggests to me that the dragonfly numbers are thinning; I saw only one this morning.

After observing numerous waves of migrating kites, I find it interesting to think that so many of them locate and use this same feeding tree. It's also interesting to consider that so many of them must be using a similar flight path as they move down from Kansas and northern Oklahoma, through the central part of the state on their way to Corpus Christi, Texas, and eventually South America. I wonder if the kites naturally follow watercourses in their migration. If not, what brings so many of them through *this* particular flight path, in which my neighborhood's trees and creek appear as a welcome stopover?

SEPTEMBER 19, 2016

After being out of state for the weekend, how nice to return to Oklahoma with its sunny skies, temperatures so warm one can still swim outdoors in comfort, and numerous Mississippi kites flying above my neighborhood and adjoining creek. Still seeing a few dragonflies and webworm larvae. Temperature today: ninety-five degrees with gentle south winds.

Saw more kites today than I have in probably two weeks. Located one juvenile kite in a blackjack tree, several feet down from the top, beneath a thick leaf canopy. It was calling steadily. While out on my morning run, I heard a kite calling and located the bird far, far up in the sky—three hundred feet or more, easily.

Its calls reached me as surely and clearly as if the bird had been perched nearby. I watched with a smile as this kite folded its wing tips and made a swift, swooping dive to a creek-side elm, where it delivered some morsel of food to its young. Humans will never achieve anywhere near the physical grace that this kite so adroitly displayed in this swift, high-altitude descent. For me, some of the most enjoyable sights in nature are these descents, some sudden and swift, others slower and gentle, whereby an adult bird glides so easily, so confidently, toward the tree limb where its offspring awaits, calling out in excitement at the sight of its parent and the promise of imminent food.

SEPTEMBER 20, 2016

No sign of the kites today, nor any sign of them yesterday afternoon after the busy kite-filled morning. Very hot. Temperature: ninety-eight degrees. Heat index: one hundred eight. Bright skies. Gentle breezes. Ragweed count very high right now. Even a walk around the block has me sneezing upon my return home. Love this weather, though it forces me to run earlier in the day, which often interferes with my work. I'm hearing a few more songbirds of a morning. I need to get out with my binoculars and see which species are migrating through central Oklahoma. From my research, Mississippi kites have been seen in Oklahoma as late in the year as October 8. I wonder how long we'll continue to see kites this year.

Storms moved through this area over the past weekend while we were gone. The high winds appear to have destroyed the kite nest in the sweetgum tree.

SEPTEMBER 22, 2016

No sign of the kites since September 19—three days now. Temperatures continue to be very warm, in the nineties, with gentle breezes from the south and sunny skies. Beautiful weather. Seeing very few fall webworms now, and no dragonflies for the past couple of days. Yesterday, noticed two pairs of robins in my backyard and have heard some beautiful singing in the woods, but haven't been able to sight the singers.

SEPTEMBER 26, 2016
No kites sighted for the past week.

SEPTEMBER 30, 2016
A few mockingbirds calling in the neighborhood now. Beautiful singing. Saw a loggerhead shrike at Hafer Park the other day. But no kites. Fall migration from my neighborhood in central Oklahoma appears to be complete. Finis.

THE POWER OF WIND

It is 2:00 A.M. and I've just opened my eyes, awakened by a sound that's part groan and part howl, potential energy driving into some confined space, intensifying its power and elevating the noise to a whirring shriek: *Zheeeeeeeeezhyoooooooo!* The storm, I tell myself. Of course. The meteorologist had warned us last evening, hours before. But it seems the meteorologists are always warning us of some impending event. And very often, nothing happens. Which is why I'd gone to bed without bringing the patio furniture indoors. I can hear the chairs being shoved around on the back porch, and that insistent shrieking noise reminding me that this time the meteorologist is correct, the leading edge of the powerful surface winds have arrived in force: *Zheeeeeeeeezhyoooooooo!*

As I lie in bed I imagine the wind funneling beneath the eaves and lifting, lifting the roof off the walls, exposing my home, my life, to the elements. Shadows of the frenetic trees in my backyard project onto the window shades like bad dreams. They seem to be made of rubber, the trees. They're leaning severely, bending and thrashing in the exorbitant breeze. It is summer, July, and I think of the nesting birds in our area, and their delicate twig and grass homes. I wonder how they can survive such merciless wind, if at all. I want to help them. I want to shelter them through the storm. But there's nothing I can do, I tell myself as I rise from bed, step onto the cool tile in the foyer, and gaze out the front windows. The river birch in my yard is taking a beating. Its branches remind me of palm fronds in a hurricane, leaves and limbs clinging so tightly together they resemble a giant brush wavering in the air on one side of the rubbery trunk. How are they still attached to the tree? How is the tree still standing? It seems the world is ending.

Zheeeeeeezhyoooooooo!

Now a garbage can comes tumbling end over end down the empty street and onto my lawn. A few seconds later it's rolling onto my front porch where, to my amazement, it collides with my door. *Thud!* The door shudders but holds. The blow rattles me. I stare out at the can, mildly aggravated and somehow reminded of a baseball meeting the thick leather of a catcher's glove. It all stops here. The force of the wind presses the garbage can against the door, which, mercifully, is made of something more substantial than leather. I'm reluctant to open it, however. The wind is too strong. I decide to leave it until morning. Besides, it's only a garbage can, and it's not going anywhere.

Blowing debris blasts the windows. I can almost feel the gritty projectiles on my cheeks and arms, and I'm reminded of another windstorm many years ago, when I was in the second grade. It came upon us during the noon recess and blew sand into our eyes. The teachers struggled to round us up and guide us back into the safety of the schoolhouse. We were momentarily blinded. We couldn't see where we were going. We placed one hand on the shoulder of the person in front of us and, using the other hand to shield our eyes from the fierce gale, marched blindly into the school, envious of those who wore glasses, our nascent minds imagining that somehow they'd been spared our wind-driven discomfort. It wasn't the teachers' fault. It wasn't anyone's fault. But I remember some of the angry parents who visited the school the following day, demanding to know why their children hadn't been ushered into the schoolhouse prior to the storm's arrival.

Recalling that long-ago windstorm, and now with a growing sense of foreboding for the river birch in my front yard, I step back from the windows, afraid of the glass shattering, grateful for my house and the shelter it provides but imagining shingles being torn from my roof, wanting to help the birds but unsure what, if anything, I can do, and wondering how many limbs, branches, trees I'm losing. My temples are throbbing. I feel short of breath. These violent storms always give me anxiety, but somehow it's worse at night. You can sense the commotion going on outdoors. You can hear it and feel it, but, like the wind itself, you can't see it.

To relax, I go into the back room, flip on the light, relieved that the power hasn't been knocked out, and turn on my stereo. I lie back on the sofa and take a deep breath as jazz notes fill the air. Dave Brubeck's thundering piano plays in counterpoint to Paul Desmond's lilting alto saxophone, and soon the wind becomes a howling accompaniment to the conversation going on between the keys and sax, the deep bass and percussive drums keeping everyone in line. Now Desmond steers the conversation into some tranquil mountain meadow, sunny and calm and filled with birdsong, his exuberant notes reminiscent of wildflowers in bloom, sweet and delicate and bursting with color. A soft place to land. I close my eyes and let the melody carry me toward morning.

————

When University of Oklahoma art professor Edith Mahier was awarded the commission to paint a mural for the Watonga, Oklahoma, post office in 1939, she probably never imagined the windstorm of criticism it would receive following its debut to the public two years later. And yet despite a letter from the Watonga postmaster to the Federal Works Agency shortly after the mural was installed in 1941, indicating that the public was pleased with the work, this is exactly what happened.

The mural, entitled *Roman Nose Canyon*, features Cheyenne

chief Henry Roman Nose, surrounded by his family in the west-ern Oklahoma canyon named for him. In the lower-left corner of the painting, three additional Cheyenne Indians are entering the canyon to water their horses. The great chief stands at the center of the composition, holding a rifle and wearing fringed leggings of deer or buffalo hide, a red breechcloth, and intricately beaded moccasins. His horse, which is drinking from the stream at his feet, wears an ornamental headstall constructed of these same decorative beads. Chief Roman Nose stands dignified and proud, though with a look of perplexity on his face. Gazing off into the distance to his right, he contemplates perhaps the future of his people and land, thoughts engendered by the scene unfolding behind him, outside the canyon on the open prairie, where white settlers have blown onto the plains. Centered directly behind the image of Chief Roman Nose is a covered wagon, a juxtaposition symbolizing two radically different lifestyles and the storm of changes to come—the arrival of European American settlers, the expansion of the West, and the resulting upheaval in the lives of the Cheyennes. Mahier's images of a man milking a cow and an axe embedded in a newly felled tree signify the impending conver-sion of the wild surroundings into an agrarian landscape, further undermining the Cheyenne way of life. And in the distance, three men stand contemplating the city they'll build, with its "churches, schools, homes, and businesses," as the artist noted.

Roman Nose Canyon depicts southern Great Plains life at the end of the nineteenth century, a tumultuous period in Oklahoma's history, and in that of the Cheyenne and other Southern Plains tribes, following the land runs that allowed white settlement of the formerly Unassigned Lands, and subsequent to President Benja-min Harrison's 1892 proclamation that opened 3.5 million acres of Cheyenne and Arapaho lands to these settlers. Ironically, this is also the year of Edith Mahier's birth.

Originally from Louisiana, Mahier graduated from Sophie Newcomb College at Tulane University in 1916, earning a bachelor's degree in design. She began teaching at the University of Oklahoma School of Art the following year. In the 1920s, Mahier traveled to Europe, becoming the first American, and first female, to study fresco painting at the Royal School of Art in Florence. Which is to say "Eli," as she was known to her students, was an accomplished artist at the time she accepted the commission to paint *Roman Nose Canyon*. Naturally, she'd gone to great lengths to ensure the cultural and historical accuracy of her mural, including consulting with anthropologists at the University of Oklahoma to learn more about Cheyenne clothing.

The U.S. Treasury Department's Section of Painting and Sculpture (later known as the Section of Fine Arts and often referred to simply as "the Section"), which had commissioned this and many other Depression-era art projects for U.S. post offices, encouraged artists to visit the communities where their works would ultimately reside to discuss potential topics with residents and to help ensure historical accuracy. Mahier found time in the spring of 1940 to visit Watonga, where she talked with local residents, both whites and Cheyenne Indians. As an artist, she knew the importance of research. She wanted to get this painting right.

Despite her efforts, however, it was a group of Cheyennes who protested *Roman Nose Canyon* in the days following its installation at the Watonga post office. It was inaccurate, they said. It was unfair, they said. It stinks, they said. Led by Roman Nose's seventy-one-year-old successor, Chief Red Bird, the Native American picketers were resolute in their condemnation of the painting, which they vowed to protest until the tribe's honor had been restored through substantial alterations to the mural. Speaking through his interpreter Joe Yellow Eyes, Chief Red Bird complained that Roman Nose's breechcloth was too short, giving him the appearance of a Navajo rather than a Cheyenne.

The protestors added that the ponies in the painting looked like "hobby horses with swan necks," and that the naked child standing beside his mother in the foreground—Roman Nose's son and heir—looked like a "stumpy pig bloated on corn meal."

Mahier's response was surprisingly upbeat: "I think a mural should arouse the interest of the people. . . . It should do that above everything. I entered the competition mainly because few Oklahoma artists were participating and they were sending out this way eastern artists who were putting English saddles on Indian ponies. At least I didn't do that."

Section officials held national and regional competitions for mural commissions. Artists submitted sketches, which were evaluated by juries of art experts and architects. Painters failing to secure a commission for a mural in one location were sometimes asked to produce one for another location if their sketches were of sufficient quality. As a result, many Oklahoma towns received murals produced by artists whose sketches had been submitted to competitions outside the state. According to the Oklahoma Historical Society, state and regional muralists created work in thirty-one Oklahoma communities between 1937 and 1942, and of the total number of Section murals created for the state, Oklahomans painted seven. Native American artists produced six of these. Edith Mahier painted the seventh.

Given the considerable research Mahier had conducted prior to and during the creation of her mural, I found it somewhat surprising that she'd offered to make revisions. After all, the artist had done her homework and had created an accurate and faithful rendering of a pivotal moment in the history of the Cheyennes, of Oklahoma, and of America's westward expansion. What possible inaccuracies might the painting reflect? Or was this offer merely a conciliatory kiss blown from Mahier's hand toward her detractors' pickets?

——

The American Wind Energy Association reports that Oklahoma, my home state, was ranked fourth in the nation in wind production as of 2016, with some 2,915 turbines and nearly 5,500 megawatts of installed wind-power capacity. Today, wind energy produces only about 4 percent of U.S. electricity, but by 2050 this number is expected to rise to 35 percent, according to the U.S. Department of Energy. Considering this, Oklahoma's wind-power capacity, like that of Texas, California, Iowa, and many other states, will most certainly increase.

Abraham Lincoln once called wind the natural force with the greatest motive power and said one of the most significant discoveries yet to be made was the taming and harnessing of it. He would be pleased at today's efforts to do exactly this.

There's a lot to love about wind . . . unlike fossil fuels, unlike power plants that rely on coal, wind power is clean . . . unlike natural gas, harnessing the wind does not involve fracking or the injection of chemically polluted wastewater into the earth . . . wind-generated electricity does not pollute the air . . . it's a domestic source of energy . . . it's a source of energy that is abundant here in the United States, and across the world . . . wind power is a sustainable form of energy . . . it provides additional income for landowners in rural areas who make their land available for the installation of wind turbines . . . the wind industry supports many jobs, seventy-three thousand of them in 2014, according to the U.S. Department of Energy . . . the energy department also tells us that by 2050 the number of wind-sector jobs related to manufacturing, installation, maintenance, and support services could exceed six hundred thousand . . . the U.S. Bureau of Labor Statistics contends that employment opportunities for wind-turbine service technicians are projected to grow by 108 percent through the year 2024, a job outlook that greatly exceeds the average for all other occupations . . . if you need a job and don't mind heights or the breeze in your face, Big Wind could be for you . . .

As with solar energy, the expenses associated with delivering wind-generated electricity have decreased significantly in recent years, so much so that solar and wind are in some markets cheaper than oil and natural gas. It's a good thing, too, because what's driving the effort to develop our clean-energy infrastructure is, of course, climate change, that great equalizer, which is already affecting all life on our planet, intensifying storms, exacerbating the melting of the Greenland ice sheets at rates that are astounding even the world's leading climate scientists, threatening polar bears and humans who make their living from hunting the ice floes, flooding South Florida neighborhoods with every full and new moon, overwhelming city infrastructures, inundating streets and parks and homes, undermining house values, displacing residents and wildlife, threating public health, threatening life on earth.

Many scientists believe it's already too late to prevent the long-anticipated effects from global warming; all we can do now, they say, is deal with the consequences. Others contend there is still a narrow margin of time remaining in which we can perhaps reduce the severity of such consequences while identifying solutions to sustain future life on planet Earth. The burgeoning wind industry is one way the United States and other countries are trying to do this, and as the debate rages between "too late" and "nearly so," the number of wind turbines continues to grow.

———

You feel exceedingly helpless and insignificant as you watch live television coverage of a tornado spinning its way toward your city, toward your town, and maybe your house. You watch the coverage and the excited team of meteorologists because to not watch would be at best irresponsible and in extreme cases almost suicidal. You watch in order to know what the tornado is doing, where it's going, and to find out whether you need to get out of the house, get out of town, go underground, or simply sit tight because the twister isn't twisting a path to your house. Unlike hurricanes, tornadoes drop from the sky suddenly. There is no time to prepare for them, no time to tape windows and tie things down. A tornado would obliterate them anyway. And once they're on the ground, these cyclones are unpredictable. They twist and turn, sometimes retracting back into the cloud that spawned them only to form again moments later.

In the absence of a storm cellar, one can often survive a small tornado by seeking shelter in the center of a house on the lowest level, inside a closet or bathroom, away from doors and windows. But the only way to survive a large tornado is to get out of its way.

Which is why, on the evening of May 3, 1999, I sat in my Oklahoma City home watching live coverage of the monster tornado tearing a path through the state as it churned toward the city like some raging bull. Unlike most tornadoes, this one had been on the ground a long time, and as it approached the Oklahoma City area it surprised everyone by continuing to strengthen. The air that day was warm and sticky, the atmosphere unsettled and windy. Conditions were perfect for a long-track tornado, and everyone knew it. Even those who ordinarily dismiss meteorologists and their predictions were tuned in to the coverage that evening. The entire city was watching and listening as the twister crossed Interstate 44 and crashed into Moore, a small municipality just south of Oklahoma City, only minutes after leveling the tiny community of Bridge Creek. Oh, no! I said as I watched the flashes of exploding electric transformers, cars being tossed into the air, and brick homes being pulverized into swirling clouds of dust and debris. Oh, no! But it was too late.

———

It's early spring and I'm on the road to the small town of Watonga, in Blaine County, in the Cheyenne and Arapaho country of western Oklahoma, to view the mural inspired by Edith Mahier's visit here seventy-eight years ago. In Mahier's time the trip might have taken several hours or more, especially for the artist herself, driving from her home in Norman. I'll do it in ninety minutes, despite a ferocious northwest wind that has me clinging to the steering wheel with both hands, one at two o'clock and the other at ten. Not long into my journey, at the junction of State Highways 3 and 4, near the small community of Piedmont, I glance off to the southwest and notice, at the top of a gentle rise, the old homestead once owned by Sarah and James McGranahan. This sun-bleached, wind-blasted home with its picturesque windmill and surrounding plains landscape was the subject of my very first published article back in 1998, when I worked as an intern for Louisa McCune, then editor in chief at *Oklahoma Today* magazine, back when the editorial offices were still located on the first floor of the elegant old Colcord Building in downtown Oklahoma City, with its marble columns, walls, and floors, and nickel-bronze letterbox and elevator doors.

Mr. McGranahan had built the home himself with wood hauled in on a wagon from what was then an obscure railroad stop just east of here, and which is today Oklahoma's largest and capital city. Early in his life, McGranahan, a settler from the East, had ridden across these plains with General George Custer. In his later years, he was appointed postmaster of Indian Territory, serving until 1889 and then operating a freight business until his retirement six years later.

In 1998 I interviewed the McGranahans' great-granddaughter, a woman named Joan Yowell, who lived nearby and who met me here to show me around the old homestead. At the time, the site seemed rural and beyond the piercing illumination of Oklahoma City traffic lights and storefronts. Today, twenty years later, as the city has continued to expand, signs of development are visible all around this once-isolated outpost. A strip mall now appears across the street in the distance, and new homes are being constructed toward the north. A new structure has even been built beside the McGranahans' old house and windmill. It's huge. It's highly conspicuous. And it's certainly incongruous with the bucolic essence of this frontier homestead. Its presence has completely obliterated the possibilities for any satisfactory photograph of this quaint quadrant of the busy intersection and its historic scene, such as the one taken by Richard Day and accompanying my brief article "The McGranahan Homestead," which appeared in the November–December 1998 issue of *Oklahoma Today.*

A few miles farther west I notice a forest of wind turbines on the horizon. As I approach these looming towers that help convert wind into electric power, I begin to feel gradually smaller and smaller. The hulking towers completely dominate the landscape here, both north and south of the highway. With today's excess wind, which is blowing steadily at thirty miles per hour and gusting to over forty, they must seem a shrewd investment of time and financial resources. However, as I approach them, these towers also appear a rather formidable barrier, especially for the birds, bats, and other wildlife that must contend with them. Just before I enter this spinning gauntlet, I notice off to my right a small house with a fenced yard. It is completely overshadowed by the wind turbines, which dominate the view to both the north and west of the house. I wonder what the home's owners think when they wake up in the morning and glance out their windows. I wonder how the birds must feel when they find these lofty, whirling obstacles in their flight paths. I wonder what Mr. McGranahan, what Chief Roman

Nose, would think if they were here today to see what has become of their former homeland.

It is nearly noon and as I pass through the tiny town of Okarche and, later, the slightly less tiny town of Kingfisher, fleets of dusty pickup trucks crowd cafés serving fried chicken and Mexican food. I drive on without stopping, hands still at ten and two on the wheel, fighting whooshing wind gusts and dodging careening eighteen-wheelers that so displace the air they feel like punches from the wind as they pass. My car vibrates and howls in the powerful air blasts.

West of Kingfisher, in a lofty elm growing near the highway, I spot the deep, heavily constructed nest of a red-tailed hawk or perhaps a great horned owl. There's no sign of these raptors, which at this point in the year may well be inside the nest with young. The surrounding biotic community, as represented in the local roadkill, includes opossum, skunk, badger, coyote, and some surprisingly large white-tailed deer. Meadowlarks dart from roadside ditches into the surrounding fields and the occasional yard. These fields, expansive and gently rolling, are blanketed in bunchgrass, bluestem, and rippling, verdant seas of winter wheat on which loll and dabble small herds of Angus cattle. Now a tumbleweed comes tumbling into view, rolling across the highway from my right to left, off the road, and then colliding with a barbed-wire fence. More trucks to dodge. Weaving, wavering, buffeting my car with their wind-driven punches. Off in the distance, the far distance, clouds of dust betray the movements and positions of such trucks as they track along the gravel-and-dirt-packed side roads, heading north, heading south, beneath the immense blue Oklahoma sky. Despite the wind, the trucks, the gritty gusts of dust that pepper my car, I find these views, the open and gently rolling land, the soaring hawks and spacious fields and sandy streams snaking beneath the highway, and the occasional stand of wind-whipped trees huddling together far off in the distance, breathtaking, and I remember just how much I adore western Oklahoma with its vast sight lines and sunshine riches, and its own brand of rawhide beauty. As Chief Roman Nose knew, this land was perfect the way it came to us, in its original and unadulterated state, and our many revisions to this natural canvas, often cited as "improvements," only detract from its authenticity. I'm grateful that most of this lovely creation survives intact.

Later, I pass a sign: Entering Cheyenne and Arapaho Nation. I begin to ascend the gypsum hills containing the canyon named for the famous Cheyenne chief, Roman Nose. The rocky hillsides are accented with cedars and oaks, which in my peripheral vision appear as green and gray brushstrokes. Soon, I'm on the summit of these low hills looking across the surrounding plains landscape over which I've just driven, and which extends unbroken as far as I can see. It occurs to me that if I were to climb out of my car and slip below the canyon rim, I'd find refuge from the incessant north wind, just as Chief Roman Nose once did.

In town I spot a sign for Watonga's historic downtown, and in no time at all I find myself climbing the steps to the city's small post office, where I sight the famous mural inside the glass doors, which are locked while the post office staff is out to lunch. The sign says the office opens again at 12:30. I have a few minutes to wait. So I stand. And wait. And glance at my watch, once, twice, and again. And then, at last, a woman appears and unlocks the door. I'm in.

Inside the small office, I stand and behold the mural. It's much larger than I anticipated, perhaps ten feet by five feet, and it's situated directly over the original, varnished wood postmaster's door. The woman is behind the counter now, serving a customer, and as she does I walk from one end of the mural to the other, taking in each individual vignette—the Cheyenne Indians entering the canyon on horseback, Chief Roman Nose himself, his family in the lower-right corner, the settlers beyond, in the background. Then I take a few steps back and consider the painting as a whole, replete with its maker's mark in the lower-left corner: Edith Mahier—1941. It occurs to me that the amount of time elapsed since completion of this beautiful oil-on-canvas mural and its installation here at the Watonga post office is the equivalent, essentially, of the average human life span. An entire hypothetical life has transpired in the succeeding years. I think of all the lives during this time that have passed through this small office beneath the eyes of Henry Roman Nose. I think, too, of the countless lives that underwent a whirlwind of change as a result of the monumental scene depicted in Edith Mahier's mural.

The customer completes his purchase, takes his sheet of stamps, and leaves the office. The post office official behind the counter—the woman who had come out to unlock the door a few moments ago, at precisely 12:30 P.M.—asks whether I need any help.

I take a deep breath. "I'm here to see the mural," I say. "I'm from Oklahoma City. I've been reading about it and thought I'd better come out and have a look."

She smiles.

"Can you tell me anything about it?"

"I bet you can probably tell me about it," she says.

I tell her what I know, which isn't much. She allows that this information is all new to her, although she has heard of the controversy and protest it spurred here in Watonga nearly eighty years ago.

"I understand it was quite a scene," she says.

———

As a young Marine serving in Saudi Arabia during the Persian Gulf War in 1991, I witnessed the sudden and terrible power of wind one afternoon when a dust devil whirled its way into our desert camp, destroying part of it. The tempest lasted only a few minutes, but it was sufficient for me to realize the power of a well-defined whirlwind, a miniature tornado of sorts. As I recall, it converted the wooden-framed shower tent and many others into piles of rumpled canvas and splinters. And though this time I had goggles to protect my eyes against blowing debris, my face and arms received an abrasive sandblasting, nevertheless.

Even this experience, however, couldn't have prepared me for what I observed when I drove through Moore, Oklahoma, on the morning of May 4, 1999.

It was surreal. It was eerie. And that's because it was so quiet. The only sounds were those of automobiles at low idle. There was no music playing. People didn't seem to be talking. Only gawking in disbelief. Stunned. Numb. Overcome with the suffocating weight of such horrific destruction. Though the interstate highway was packed that morning, as we approached Moore everyone seemed to forget that they were in a hurry to get to work and school. Traffic crawled through the minefield of debris scatted along the highway. The puzzle pieces of rubble that had been homes only the day before now littered the roadside and a nearby field. There was an enormous gouge in the near distance, on either side of the highway, like a shallow canyon. It was the earth-scarring groove the tornado had left when it came through and swept homes right off their foundations. These cement foundations were now clean and bare. As I recall, the crater was perhaps a hundred yards wide, and it continued for as far as I could see to the west. On either side of it were oceans of debris and people wading through it in disbelief, as well as fleets of police cars and emergency vehicles and gangs of news reporters.

As I neared the end of the debris field I steered my car around a sofa sitting on the edge of the interstate. It was situated in such a way that it seemed its owner might be in the next room making a snack or preparing to return to the comfort of its cushions, which appeared unscathed.

Twenty years later, no one who lived through it has forgotten the "May Third Tornado": an F5 monster that killed forty-four people, destroyed more than three hundred homes in central Oklahoma, and produced wind velocities exceeding three hundred miles per hour, the highest wind speeds ever recorded.

———

Saturday dawns cold and rainy, but because I'm in New York City I don't mind at all. I rise, shower and shave, and after breakfast head over to Fifth Avenue, to the Metropolitan Museum of Art, where I spend hours admiring nineteenth- and early twentieth-century European paintings by the likes of Matisse, Cézanne, Renoir, Gauguin, and, in Gallery 822, works by Vincent van Gogh.

Weaving my way through the crowds I soon spot his *Wheat Field with Cypresses* displayed on its own wall. Isolated as it is, and resplendent in its precise illumination, the painting, with its heavily impastoed brushstrokes and vibrant colors, seems to live and breathe. All my life I've been partial to the juxtaposition, to the complementary pairing, of the colors blue and yellow. It doesn't matter what form it takes; when I spot this color pairing on clothes, art, book covers, furniture, even food, I gravitate to it. In *Wheat Field with Cypresses*, van Gogh has given us variations on these hues, with the field of golden grains in the foreground and the swirling azure (and white) sky beyond. But even more than these exuberant colors, for me, is the suggestion of movement in this work. The wheat stalks sway like a kelp forest in a strong ocean current. The olive trees, too, seem equally caressed by the zephyr, while the blue-and-white sky, with its swirling clouds and thermals, is vibrant and arresting. I don't know what anyone else sees when they view *Wheat Field with Cypresses*, but when I gaze at this painting I see movement. I feel the wind exerting its forces on the landscape, gold, green, and lush, transcending time and space, coating the chattering crowd in a cloud of reverential hush.

Van Gogh had checked himself into a mental asylum at Saint-Rémy-de-Provence, in southern France, in the spring of 1889. He was living there when he completed *Wheat Field with Cypresses*. During this time he also produced several other landmark works, including his famous nocturnal scene *The Starry Night*. One of the great ironies of van Gogh and his paintings from this period is that he produced some of the Western world's most recognized and revered artwork during one of the most psychiatrically dark and volatile periods of his life. It's remarkable that he was able to capture so much light and color and movement—and *life*—at a time when his own was in such jeopardy. Perhaps sensing his own mortality provided the inspiration he needed to produce his best work.

———

Located a few miles northwest of Watonga, and opened in 1937, is one of Oklahoma's original state parks. Like the canyon that bears his name, this park too was named after Henry Roman Nose, the great Cheyenne warrior chief, and was only a few years old when Edith Mahier's mural was installed at the Watonga post office in 1941, a time when the effects of the Great Depression were still being felt across the nation. Perhaps it was for this reason that city leaders devised the idea for a Native American–led protest of the painting as a way to garner media attention for Roman Nose State Park (and, by extension, the town of Watonga) as a tourist destination. The plan seems to have worked, as newspapers from the East covered the event while Americans everywhere followed the protests through daily radio broadcasts.

Amid the picketing and bickering and general unrest swirling through the hot air in western Oklahoma in June 1941, Mahier wrote a letter to Section assistant chief Edward Rowan, inform-ing him she'd received a note from an assistant at the *Watonga*

Republican, advising her not to worry, that the protest was simply a publicity stunt and that everyone knew it. "In fact, it'll probably make you more famous than you already are," the note read.

Shortly thereafter, the picketers went home and the controversy seemed to dissipate, for in the end the only thing of substance was Edith Mahier's mural, which can still be viewed today.

———

The sounds of singing birds awaken me. I open my eyes, momentarily confused, wondering why I'm lying on the sofa in the back room. Then a new Brubeck song begins and I recall the storm, the stereo I've left playing all night. Later, and much to my surprise, I'll rise and find only a few stray leaves scattered about my yard and driveway, and I'll feel no small relief from the realization that the heavy gusts from last night, though they sounded much worse, were mercifully more bluff than bite.

But for now, I resolve to enjoy a few more minutes on the sofa listening to the Dave Brubeck Quartet. I love Mr. Brubeck's piano, but it's Paul Desmond's saxophone that really puts me in my groove. *Time Out*, the album I'm listening to, is one of Brubeck's masterpieces. Each of the seven songs features a unique time signature. Yet it was Brubeck's friend and sideman Paul Desmond who composed the album's pièce de résistance, the song that would eventually become the biggest-selling jazz single ever: "Take Five," a spellbinding number with a mesmerizing melody and intriguing drum solo.

At a time when many aspiring alto saxophone players sought to emulate Charlie Parker's aggressive bebop style, Desmond resolved to develop his own signature and ended up creating one of the most unique sounds in jazz, a light, melodic style that Desmond himself once compared to a dry martini.

Of all his work, "Audrey," a song Desmond recorded with Dave Brubeck in 1955 as part of the studio record *Brubeck Time*, is my absolute favorite. The notes from his saxophone are light and languid, but sharply insistent. It's a sweet song. It's a melancholy song. It's a song whose title pays homage to the actress Audrey Hepburn, the thought of whom sauntering out of the woods and drifting toward him, the story goes, caused Desmond's eyes to glaze over as the band prepared to record her namesake tribute, one moment stopping the great jazzman cold, and the next inspiring one of countless performances over the years that would elevate him into the pantheon reserved for only the heaviest names in jazz saxophone: Charlie Parker, Lucky Thompson, John Coltrane, and a half note of others.

Paul Desmond died in 1977 at the young age of fifty-two, a giant of modern jazz. Though he had mastered the alto saxophone, developing a style and sound unlike any other, time also rendered him, tragically, a victim of cancer. After decades of chain smoking, his lungs, which had propelled him to fame, finally had nothing left to give. And that's where the music stopped.

IT NOURISHES YOU

Her eyelids flutter a moment and then fade. Her svelte body shudders to the metronome rhythm of respiration, involuntary respiration, each breath quick and shallow and steady: inhale, exhale . . . expand, contract . . . inhale, exhale. . . . Again her eyes flicker, sticky eyelids, reluctant to part, peeling open, blinking, blinking, and then slowly closing. Inhale, exhale . . . expand, contract . . . inhale, exhale . . .

It's a sunny and cool December morning in Oklahoma, and a Bewick's wren is calling from the edge of the woods. A tufted titmouse flutters through the limbs of an ash tree as a pair of Carolina chickadees, dropping from branch to branch like feathered raindrops, descend onto the feeder in my backyard, which is brimming with sunflower seeds. Nearby, and indifferent to these seeds, a downy woodpecker hammers its way along the limb of a blackjack oak, its steady percussive song the sound of confidence, independence. The morning is calm, and the few leaves remaining on the trees cling precariously to the glories of the rapidly departing year. In the meadow across the creek, the bluestem and switchgrass gleam in the rising sun, awaiting the white-tailed deer soon to come bounding through, or a tawny bobcat skulking the creek banks, long legged, lithe, and silent as it hunts for a rabbit or a bird like the little goldfinch on the ground before me.

She's blinking again. Eyelids as delicate as wildflower petals part reluctantly, briefly, and then close as she fades back into her dazed dream. Now two tiny feathers flutter softly to the ground like yellow snowflakes, having lost their sticky purchase on the plate-glass window with which my little golden girl has just collided. Behind me, I hear the birds scratching through the seeds in the feeder and flying away. Without turning to look, I picture the scene: perched on the ash limb nearby, each bird waiting its turn to drop onto the feeder, and then descending, one by one by one, the cardinals eating in, the chickadees and titmice and juncos taking their meals to go. Some of the birds scratch out a good bit of the seed, which is soon claimed by others on the ground. Whenever this happens I wonder who's feeding whom.

Now her dark eyes remain open for several seconds, shining in the soft morning light, revealing the delicate but resilient life within. Her breathing, still quick and steady, her posture stable, I hesitate to pick her up and decide instead to just sit and watch her regain her faculties, knowing that although my house and its glass windows may be impeding the birds' flight paths to some extent, at least I'm protecting her from the sharp-shinned hawks that swoop in suddenly from time to time, the prowling bobcats along the creek, and certainly free-roaming house cats.

Sometimes I think it might be preferable to remove the feeders in my backyard and allow the birds to fend for themselves, although I prefer to believe they're benefiting from the suet and sunflower seeds I provide them during the lean winter months. Yet as I sit here watching the little golden girl slowly come to her senses, I have my doubts. And I wonder: Am I doing this for the birds, or my own enjoyment? The answer, of course, is both. But why should one—in this case, the feeding—detract from the other or, worse, prove in any way detrimental to the birds? To my way of thinking, it shouldn't. That's certainly not my intent. Nor is it, I imagine, the intent of any of the fifty-two million Americans who feed birds and other wildlife around their homes. But the American Goldfinch on the ground before me suggests otherwise, and this is what I'm struggling with. How do we benefit our wild neighbors without adversely impacting them through the very same actions, however benevolent in spirit? How do we benefit the natural world that so enriches our lives, and which we're part of, without simultaneously damaging it? How unobtrusive must I make myself, how insignificant must my presence on this earth be, simply to have a *neutral* effect? Is this even possible? The probability that it's not is troubling, disorienting. I rub my forehead in an attempt to ward off the migraine I feel coming on.

A 2015 report from the *Proceedings of the National Academy of Sciences* detailed a study in which researchers in New Zealand spent eighteen months analyzing the effects of supplemental feeding on urban bird communities. Using monthly bird surveys to determine avian community composition and species density at twenty-three residential properties, including both feeding and nonfeeding stations, the researchers found that bird populations diverged in those locations where supplemental feeding occurred. More importantly, they found that such feeding tended to benefit nonnative species—in this case, the house sparrow and spotted dove—while having a negative effect on native insectivores, such as the gray warbler. Though research indicates that these imbalances tend to desist once supplemental feeding ceases, it nevertheless reveals that feeding contributes substantially to the structure of urban bird communities, potentially altering the balance between native and nonnative species.

Why is this of concern? Ask any ecologist and he or she will tell you that invasive species, whether plant, mammal, fish, or bird, gradually displace native flora and fauna. Eventually, this unnatural displacement is multiplied across the food chain and its effects felt throughout all levels of the ecosystem.

Curious about the larger ecological implications of bird feeding, particularly that resulting from species imbalance, I contacted the lead researcher of the study, Josie Galbraith, a biologist at the University of Auckland, in New Zealand. Josie told me that because most studies to date have been conducted in very specific areas, on limited scales, drawing conclusions about larger impacts is difficult. She pointed out, however, that the homogenization of urban bird communities brought about through supplemental feeding could have other, secondary effects. "If pollinating birds are losing out, and are displaced by other non-pollinators, then there could be an impact on regeneration of plants and trees," she told me. "This doesn't have to be a native [versus] nonnative issue though. It could occur within communities of purely native birds too."

Which could, once again, lead to an unnatural species imbalance, potentially affecting the larger ecosystem. Given this, one can imagine a scenario in which mosquito-eating birds, for instance, could be displaced by noninsectivores, which could result in the proliferation of these disease-carrying insects. This could potentially have consequences for human health, especially where such imbalances occur across large regions, and for extended periods. In light of this, one wonders about the current Zika outbreak in South Florida (and elsewhere, in Latin America and the Caribbean). Scientists tell us that the *Aedes aegypti* mosquito, the vector for the Zika virus, is an urban insect that lives close to human habitations, thriving in our garbage, breeding in our birdbaths and the water bowls we set out for our pets, even living inside our homes. But beyond this, what other factors are contributing to its proliferation? Is it simply an abundance of habitat? Or has the *Aedes aegypti* mosquito somehow benefited from a lack of predation resulting from a similar imbalance of insect-eating bird species in these areas, one brought about through human activity such as habitat destruction, urban or suburban development, or perhaps something as innocuous as bird feeding?

There is simply not enough evidence to answer these questions at this point.

In the meantime, I resolve to continue feeding the birds because I want to believe that despite the occasional mishap, despite whatever detrimental effects occur from time to time, my efforts— and those of kindred spirits all across the world—are ultimately benefiting them. Food is scarce during winter, and in supplementing their diets we're helping them through these difficult months, even as they nourish us through the color and life they lend to an otherwise bleak off-season landscape. One suspects—and I'm sure many bird-watchers would agree—that the psychological and spiritual sustenance we derive from feeding birds is equivalent to the physical benefits birds receive from the suet and seeds we provide. And in this sense our relationship is symbiotic.

Perhaps we're also contributing to the greater good, to something more significant and enduring than our own small lives, something we can't quite quantify but feel in our hearts and minds.

Growing up, my brothers and I spent a lot of time with our maternal grandmother. She had lived through the Great Depression. The hardships she'd experienced weren't often mentioned, but they manifested themselves in a number of ways, such as the leftover food she saved, the pantry of nonperishables she maintained, and her fruit trees and vegetable garden, the products of which she canned and collected on her cellar's shelves. Perhaps most indicative of her experiences, as well as the considerable value she placed on food, was her compassion for the hungry and a willingness to share with and feed anyone in need. My grandmother helped me understand in no uncertain terms that the meaning of wealth, and that sense we know as "security," has nothing to do with money, large homes, or new cars. Rather, it has everything to do with food, being able to feed yourself, having enough to eat. If one is hungry, I realized, then everything becomes subservient to that hunger, and nothing else really matters. On the other hand, when our hunger is appeased we're free to engage the larger world, free to pursue our lives and dreams. This makes anything possible.

While these lessons came early in life, eventually I grew to realize that food is something more than simple fuel to carry us through the day. Eating not only satisfies our appetites, providing the nourishment necessary to sustain us, it also feeds our minds and souls. Foods' flavors and textures and aromas, and their many associated pleasures, are part of the joy of being human. Playwright George Bernard Shaw famously said that there is no love sincerer than the love of food, an observation that recognizes both the physical necessity of eating and, perhaps equally, the emotional sustenance we derive from the same. Among other things, the foods we eat tell us who we are, where we come from, and something about the world we live in. Eating, then, is a way of identification. It's also a means of connecting with others. I'm reminded of this every time my wife and I prepare dinner using one of my grandmother's old recipes. Eating a piece of pumpkin pie, for example, made with her delectable crust, is essentially to go back in time. The flavors trigger the picture show in my mind, and as I eat I'm instantly transported decades into the past, to my grandmother's kitchen, where I sit at her table, warm and secure, relishing those very same flavors.

In his book *The Physiology of Taste*, Jean Anthelme Brillat-Savarin spoke to food's timeless and enduring charms, noting, "The pleasure of the table belongs to all ages, to all conditions, to all countries, and to all æras; it mingles with all other pleasures, and remains at last to console us for their departure."

But if the foods we eat tell us who we are, then what can be said of that which we provide to others? What does this reveal about us?

In sharing food, in feeding the hungry, even on the smallest and simplest of terms, my grandmother introduced me to the concept of noblesse oblige, which, though seldom mentioned today, has endured through the years, less a product of tradition, I believe, than one stemming from our abiding moral compass. Deep down in all of us is a desire to assist, to care for, to nurture others, even other species. These traditions are as old as humanity. It's part of who we are. Emily Dickinson spoke to this compulsion in her poem "Not in Vain": "If I can stop one heart from breaking / I shall not live in vain."

Whenever I watch the cardinals and chickadees gathering around my backyard feeders, sometimes I can still see my grandmother preparing a sandwich for a drifter, breaking up slices of bread and tossing these pieces to the robins in her yard, or placing a pan of leftovers on her back porch for the stray dog that had wandered up to her house. Food was offered not in pity but out of respect, compassion, and an understanding that life can be so hard, that we're all going through this big world together, and that it's our duty to care enough to share, to help those in need, every living thing.

Of course, I derive no small amount of pleasure from feeding the birds around my house, and, in being thus attuned to my local bird communities, I'm more involved and invested in their welfare, as well as that of the larger ecosystem. After all, observing nature, immersing ourselves in it, and learning about it are the first steps toward protecting it. And if we can do this, we will not have lived in vain.

———

Ask any hundred bird watchers why they do what they do, and you're likely to receive as many different responses. I am reminded of one particular retort to this recurring question, which appeared in the form of an April 2002 article in the *Christian Science Monitor*.

The author of the article, Robert Winkler, notes that those of us who watch birds do so for one simple reason: because they're here. "Yes, they control insects," he writes, "but their benefit to humanity is no more the measure of their worth than the pharmacy shelf is the measure of the tropical rain forest. Wildlife has a right to exist for its own sake."

My spirits were buoyed by this observation, as well as by Winkler's assessment that the real fascination in watching birds stems from the freedom and wildness they embody, about which humans can only dream. "I think we envy the birds' wild freedom," he writes. "We want that freedom and wildness for ourselves. And so we birders watch, listen to, identify, count, list, house, feed, and photograph birds."

A plausible explanation, certainly, for this is precisely the reason so many of us watch sports. Most people lack the athletic prowess that could place us in league with high-level sports figures. For this reason we're often enthralled by those who possess such gifts, the ability to run, throw, dive, lean, and leap beyond the boundaries that bind most of us to less dramatic lives. But even the most common birds possess gifts, and freedoms, that are simply unattainable to humans.

Such freedom was never more beautifully displayed than last summer, as I undertook a close study of the Mississippi kites in my area. Each day I would watch these beautiful raptors soar through the bright blue Oklahoma skies, catching cicadas, grasshoppers, and dragonflies, which the adults would then deliver to their nests to feed their rapidly growing young. Sometimes this occurred with a gentle, low-altitude glide into the nest. Other times, the adult kites would fold their wings and descend suddenly from three or four hundred feet in the sky, angling sharply and at high speed, only to expand their wings at the final moment, land deftly on the edge of their nest, deliver the morsel, and take to the skies once again in the kind of ceaseless and seemingly thankless pursuit that only a parent can know. In all cases, when a fledgling would spot its parent arriving with food, whether from thirty or three hundred feet away, its call would change from a sporadic cry into a steady, high-pitched whine like that of a puppy, which abated only after the adult's arrival at the nest. Six months later, though the kites have all left for the year, I can still hear these fledglings calling in excitement at the sight of their elegant and graceful parents bringing food, nourishment, security. Thinking back forty years, I remember exactly how that feels.

———

She tilts her gaze to the left, now to the right, her brown eyes clear and bright. Now she turns her head. Does she see me? Do I frighten her? Or does she somehow understand that my presence, my intentions, are purely altruistic? Her breathing remains steady, quick and even and steady. I admire her soft downy head, her golden-yellow throat, the way her jutting tail feathers terminate in a neatly symmetrical fork—a form and function that humans can strive to replicate, but in my opinion never duplicate, never surpass or improve upon. Mother Nature is perfect the way she is, and that's the beauty in all this. And also the tragedy. As a global society, we must commit ourselves fully and wholeheartedly to protecting and preserving the natural world, not just because it's sublime, not only because it brings beauty and joy and meaning to our lives, but because it's irreplaceable.

Yesterday morning while driving home after taking my son to school, I had just passed a deer-crossing sign the city had erected, warning drivers to pay heed, when a red-tailed hawk dropped from a tree and glided low over the road directly in front of me, maintaining this dramatic but dangerous low-altitude trajectory until reaching a tree in a field across the roadway, at which point it swooped up to a perch on a dead branch. It was a beautiful sight, and for a few precious seconds I flew vicariously with the hawk, possessing a bird's-eye view of the road and adjoining field. I could almost feel the hawk's focus as it glided so smoothly and effortlessly through the air in front of me. The encounter might have been very different, however, had I come along just a moment sooner, or had I been driving, as so many motorists in this area do, much more quickly. It reminded me of the narrow margins in which we live our lives. It reminded me too of Chief Seattle, the ancient leader of the Duwamish and Suquamish tribes, who once observed that if all the beasts disappeared from the earth, humans would die of a great loneliness of the spirit, for all life is connected. In watching the hawk sail across the roadway in front of me, in feeding the birds around my house, I understand what he was saying.

The birds are alighting on the feeder behind me, snatching sunflower seeds, flying away to crack them open. The breeze rustles the leaves in the trees and suddenly my little golden girl snaps to life. She darts away, porpoising through the air toward a nearby oak, where she alights, animated and vivacious as she skitters along the limb, surveying her surroundings. Then she spins and falls away from the tree as she descends on the feeder, where it's my hope she'll find something nourishing enough to continue to call my backyard home, at least through the winter.

CPSIA information can be obtained
at www.ICGtesting.com
Printed in the USA
LVHW091301180220
647317LV00002B/240